ROSY GLASSES

Kazuo Ozaki in 1973   *Photo: Robert Epp*

ROSY GLASSES

&
OTHER STORIES

by
Kazuo Ozaki

TRANSLATED FROM THE
JAPANESE AND INTRODUCED

by
ROBERT EPP

Paul Norbury Publications /UNESCO
Woodchurch Ashford Kent

UNESCO COLLECTION OF REPRESENTATIVE WORKS
Japanese Series

THIS WORK FROM THE JAPANESE HAS BEEN ACCEPTED IN
THE TRANSLATIONS COLLECTION SPONSORED BY THE
UNITED NATIONS EDUCATIONAL, SCIENTIFIC AND
CULTURAL ORGANIZATION (UNESCO).

First published 1988 by
PAUL NORBURY PUBLICATIONS LTD
Woodchurch, Ashford, Kent, England
ISBN 0-904404-52-8

British Library Cataloguing in Publication Data

Ozaki, Kazuo
    Rosy glasses & other stories.— (Unesco Collection of
Representative Works. Japanese series).
    I. Title II. Series
    895.6′34[F] PL835.Z3

    ISBN 0-904404-52-8

*This book has been set in Plantin roman
10 on 11½ point by Visual Typesetting and
printed & bound by A. Wheaton & Co Ltd
of Exeter, England*

Contents

Introduction

MARCEL PROUST CLAIMED that he had not 'created' one of his early autobiographical stories, he had 'harvested' it. The same might be said of these stories by Ozaki Kazuo, who 'harvests' only what happens to him, only what he knows from direct involvement with life. At times he embroiders with fictive elements some episode he has experienced or some character appearing in the story — the more accurately to convey the truth of what he has seen and felt. From the very first, however, Ozaki — who takes ultimate reality to be personal experience and the welter of day-to-day events — has assiduously avoided any imposition of abstract or artificial structure on the data of life. This means that his stories clearly fall into the I-novel category and that his approach to writing reflects certain traditional aesthetic values.

In fact, many Ozaki stories represent a typically indigenous variation of the I-novel genre. Japanese literary critics call this sub-category *shinkyō shōsetsu*, a term that appears frequently enough in discussions of this author's work to warrant a brief explanation here. Simply speaking, *shinkyō shōsetsu* means 'a story of the state of the *kokoro.*' The *shin* of *shinkyō*, the Sinic reading of the graph for *kokoro*, means heart or mind: what makes the human being human. *Kokoro* suggests will, knowledge, sentiment, and the like — qualities moderated by the emotional rather than the rational dimensions of the psyche. Critics generally associate this type of I-novel with the main works of Ozaki and his mentor, Shiga Naoya (1883-1971). Indeed, they invariably list as models of the genre Shiga's *At Kinosaki* (1917) and Ozaki's *This and That About Bugs* (1948). And they add that the *shinkyō shōsetsu's* basic characteristics, all of which I regard as more traditional than modern, include the protagonist's sense of crisis and attempts to resolve it, his drive to alleviate some psychological problem that stymies him, or efforts to develop self-control and overcome private inconsistencies so as to achieve harmony with others.

In a far broader sense, this sub-category of the I-novel contains both modern and traditional elements. In its modern aspects, we can consider the *shinkyō shōsetsu* a Japanese-style contemplative or reflective novel. It closely approaches what Goethe calls the subjective novel, in which the author muses over incidents in his life to reveal

the atmosphere of his mind, his *shinkyō*. In Ozaki's hands, this story
deals basically with extremely personal and psychological data as it
celebrates seemingly insignificant details of daily life, particularly
events that occur in the author's home. These characteristics connect
his work with traditional Japanese approaches to story writing.

In Japan, the traditional aesthetic assumes that art should deal
with what lies closest to actual experience, with what the artist feels
most intensely. That is, emotions count far more than intellect. One
aspect of this aesthetic holds that true art or true beauty exists
essentially in the minute and the everyday, in what is natural and
spontaneous. Art is, in short, not the result of what the author
artificially plots or organises in his mind. Ideas of this sort characterise
the work of many story-tellers throughout history, in Japan and
elsewhere, who prefer to describe life as it happens without artificially
creating climaxes and resolutions of tensions. Such writers maintain,
like Ozaki, that daily life itself provides literature with an adequate
context without forcing experience to become a stage where an author
manipulates his characters by the principles of cause and effect. That
is to say, writers like Ozaki define 'plot' as that which naturally
happens to the writer, not what he makes his characters do.

To treat private experience and life's seemingly unimportant
daily events as art itself, rather than simply as the sources of art,
does not detract from Ozaki's ability to analyse his psyche or confess
his faults. He can act like any modern I-novelist without, in fact,
writing a psychological novel or a 'realistic confessional' in the purely
western sense. His I-novels contain elements resembling those found
in western forms without properly fitting into either category. It is,
for example, quite clear that neither Ozaki's sense of crisis nor his
personal revelations originate in his desire to withdraw from society.
Nor does he retreat into the personal novel because he hates social
institutions, because he feels disgust and impotence, because he
wants to alleviate feelings of alienation and rage, or because he
laments a radical breakdown in community — all standard
motivations for the realistic confessional novelist in the West.

Although Ozaki's work frequently does reflect a modern
awareness of the self, the way he uses confessional materials to reveal
that self seems comparatively traditional. The modern dimension
emerges in disclosures of private events and feelings that suggest his
desire to reduce psychological tensions or attain a clearer perception
of his essential being, his innermost self. But his reasons for solving
psychic tensions or achieving better self-understanding betray a
strong traditional colouration. He does not lament psychological
tautness or the disintegration of the only world he has, he seeks ways
to overcome tensions so as to improve or rebuild that world. Unlike

the usual modern western confessional writer, we do not sense Ozaki's motivation is self-centered because he aims to achieve concord with his immediate environment. Everywhere in his stories the commitment to improving the quality of his being echoes the indigenous urge for harmony (*wa*), an urge decidedly informed by moral concerns. These concerns are moral in the sense that Ozaki wishes both to improve himself as a person and to consider what consequences his behaviour, thoughts, and decisions might have on his life and on the lives of those closest to him.

His reasons for writing about himself and his family are basically affirmative, and they reflect unselfish moral concerns for self-improvement that contrast markedly with confessional realistic writers. Not only does Ozaki avoid giving the impression that he wishes to shock his readers, he never indulges in the seamy or titillating detail that so often characterises the style of the realistic writer. Ozaki, moreover, finds this style of writing — whether confessional in the academic sense or not — the most natural and authentic way to express himself. He says wryly that writing private stories about himself and his immediate family saves him a good deal of worry; with tongue in cheek, he claims his models cannot complain about how he depicts them in his stories.

Ozaki does not object to critics labelling his stories *shinkyō shōsetsu*. We should nevertheless keep in mind that at no time in his career has he ever consciously written one. He simply harvests experience. For him, reality is not taxonomy; it is life. One cannot deny that the term serves as a handy tag to designate Ozaki's explorations of life, his interaction with self and family members, and the way he mulls over events experienced in his home. But taxonomy should not replace analysis of how this writer puts his stories together. That would be to fall into the familiar trap of dealing with problems merely by defining them. The aim of this essay is neither to define *shinkyō shōsetsu* nor to decide whether Ozaki's stories aptly fit that category. The task is rather to discuss the most basic characteristics of his art and thus communicate an understanding of his aesthetic. Besides, no label can possibly suggest the intensely personal dimension of this author's stories: Ozaki is the tale, the tale is Ozaki.

Coming to terms with a style of writing that is so personal requires background knowledge. Not only must we know something about the author's life, we must understand his artistic methods as well. Lack of information in either area makes it altogether too easy to categorise his work, and seize on a condescending statement of dismissal by referring to him as, at most, a 'genial chronicler of impoverished but happy domesticity.' If we are to be fair, before criticising him we must at least confront the fundamental issues that frame his work. This done, we may in the end choose neither to applaud nor to recognise as literature this writer's efforts, and may indeed agree that Ozaki is, after all, no more than a 'genial chronicler.' On the other hand, by looking carefully at his work and by gaining some insight into the aesthetic behind his stories, the chances are that the ready-made tags that overlook or downplay the merit of his work will seem less than adequate.

Two of the following four sections introduce selected details of Ozaki's life. The first describes the origin of tensions with his family. I deal here mainly with the time from his mid-teens to his last year at college. The second section touches particularly on his poverty and the launching of his literary career. These sections suggest how closely Ozaki's life parallels his stories by providing basic information against which to view descriptions of his youthful years in the stories themselves. Because all the works in this collection accurately describe the author's life experiences, one may say that his art reflects so vividly his personal life that Ozaki the man is never absent from the core of any story. Unlike true fiction, then, what he writes here commands no genuine existence independent of the person and the personal life of the author. Indeed, even when Ozaki writes objectively about the adventures of his persona, Ogata Shōkichi, the author behind the mask always remains a powerful force dominating the content and organisation of each story.

In the two remaining sections, I identify five fundamental features that characterise Ozaki's work. Part III describes three aspects of self-awareness — everywhere moderated by a commitment to authenticity — that influence his choice of details: the urge for self-examination as he attempts to comprehend experience; a desire for harmony and belonging that focuses attention on familial relationships; and a thirst for self-improvement, a profoundly moral concern for character development emerging from the desire to understand the self and get along with those closest to him. Part IV describes two attitudes that deeply affect the way Ozaki structures the raw material of experience: regarding the self as the story to be told, he rejects all artificial means of organising what happens to him; furthermore, he believes that description of life should be structured mainly by the natural unities of existence, by various rhythmic repetitions that reflect experience itself. In my judgement, knowledge of these five points comprises the minimum requirement for making a sound evaluation of Ozaki's achievement.

I

Knowledge of Ozaki's family background explains many early tensions with his father and, later, his family. He was not yet twenty in 1918 when his father died, leaving him the head of the household: upholder of Ozaki traditions and guardian of the family property. For generations the family had been associated with a Shinto shrine near the ancestral residence in Shimosoga, not far from Odawara in Kanagawa Prefecture. Thanks to the meticulous genealogical records his Shinto priest forebears kept, Ozaki traces his ancestry back more than five hundred years. His father, Yatsuka, departed slightly from the priestly tradition by becoming a professor of history at the Shinto seminary in Ise. Ozaki's mother, Tai, was the second daughter of a Shinto priest also noted as a scholar of classical Japanese. Yatsuka had married while still a student at Tokyo Imperial University and Tai became pregnant before he graduated. As the first son, Ozaki fell heir to all the pressures and expectations usually laid on the shoulders of the scion of a well-established traditional family.

In his mid-teens, however, he fell in love with literature. Unfortunately, most conservative people from a good family background in those days considered writing 'frivolous stories' an inappropriate activity, especially for the heir. Inevitably, considerable friction developed once his father discovered his commitment. Ozaki began with classical poetry, a harmless enough hobby. But during the summer of 1916 when gastric problems forced Yatsuka to take early retirement from the seminary, Ozaki happened to read *Ōtsu Junkichi*, a confessional story by Shiga Naoya. This novel — which catalogues some of the problems with an awakening sexuality that Ōtsu Junkichi, Shiga's *alter ego*, experienced as a young man —deeply impressed the then sixteen-year-old Ozaki. For the first time he saw how, using only personal experience, a writer might explore the meaning of life or find a modern definition of person in an essentially feudal milieu. This not only reflected what he felt the novel should be but confirmed his wish to become such a writer. As far as his father was concerned, however, such writing was far worse than merely turning out 'frivolous stories.' It was demeaning: Yatsuka considered confessional novels no more than works by wastrels or degraded authors who were seeking to entertain women. Certainly no heir of a respectable family would write material like that.

Ozaki's desire to enter Waseda College in Tokyo compounded the friction between him and his father. Few decisions could have displeased Yatsuka more. A staunch supporter of conservative values and Tokyo University, he detested Waseda, a school he associated with liberal and anti-Establishment values. A maverick statesman had founded Waseda in 1881 to provide an alternative to the state-centred education offered at Tokyo Imperial University, which was weighted towards the training of bureaucrats. Thus, from the outset Waseda's reputation as a hot-bed of anti-government activities encouraged the stereotype that malcontents and radicals dominated the college. The fact was that by providing advanced training for those interested in fields like law and writing, whether journalism, novels, or poetry, the school served an extremely useful function. That did not prove sufficient justification, however, for Yatsuka to allow his first son to study there.

Ozaki's father demanded instead that he prepare to enter the First Higher School, the élite route to Tokyo University. But having spent much of the time during his last years at the five-year local middle school writing *haiku* and *tanka*, Ozaki's academic foundations were very shaky to say the least. Not only was he ill prepared to compete with the intellectuals struggling to get into such a prestigious school, he did no more than go through the motions of studying for the exam. All along he continued to write and submit poetry to magazines — a fact his father discovered by accident when the postman delivered a prize he had won for one of his verses. That made it impossible to conceal the fact that he was not wholeheartedly studying for his exams. Naturally, in due course, he failed with flying colours!

Although Kazuo did not pass the exam, in effect closing the door to Tokyo University, Yatsuka refused to give in to Ozaki's passion for writing. In the end, however, he did allow his son to take classes at another Tokyo school, thus allowing him to remain in the capital. The proviso was that he would not study literature. Outwardly obedient and feigning acquiescence, Ozaki promptly went about doing as he pleased. He justified his disobedience by claiming that the nature of the modern novel differed utterly from his father's misconceptions; it would no longer be considered a mere toy to titillate women or weaklings. Indeed, seeing it as a tool to uncover the self and understand experience, Ozaki ensconced himself in a library near campus and read all the literature he could get his hands on. Rarely attending class, he also had time to submit classical poetry to journals and to dream of writing something confessional like Shiga's *Ōtsu Junkichi*. During the first months at Hōsei, Ozaki also spent a good deal of time attending vaudeville shows and popular dramas, hardly the activities Yatsuka would prefer his son and heir to engage in.

At the height of tension with his father, the world-wide Spanish flu epidemic following World War I suddenly claimed Yatsuka's life.

Once Ozaki recovered from the shock of his father's death, he experienced an exhilarating sense of freedom and power. He had become the head of the family and could decide his own future. But freedom also brought the onus of responsibility and duty. Ozaki felt anxious to exploit his powers but not at all eager to discharge his duties as the head of the household, as he soon made clear. One week after his father's funeral he announced to his mother rather brazenly that he would transfer from Hōsei to Waseda. She turned visibly pale but said nothing. Nor could she, for in the traditional family of that time the first son, on the death of his father, inherited all the father's authority; this meant the widow must obey her son as she had obeyed her husband. Only moments before Ozaki's announcement, he and his mother had finished inspecting the contents of the camphor-wood box he would mention later in the story entitled Land of My Fathers. There they discovered Yatsuka's records of property, stocks, bonds, and savings the family owned. Clearly, there were enough resources to allow all five children a considerable amount of education beyond the compulsory six years.

Ozaki's next hurdle was the entrance examination to Waseda Academy, the most direct route to Waseda College. For the first time in his life, he systematically applied himself to his studies and passed the exam. But the long feud with his father over their contrasting philosophies of life, the turmoil following Yatsuka's death, and the strain of preparing for the entrance examination apparently took their toll. During his first year at the Academy, Ozaki contracted tuberculosis. In those days, TB often amounted to a death sentence; unlike cancer, it is a communicable disease, so he can hardly be blamed for describing his illness euphemistically as a 'severe case of pleurisy.' During his year-long convalescence in Shimosoga, his younger sister, Sei, died of the disease, which had spread to her lungs from her liver. She had just turned twenty. Within a two-year span, Ozaki had experienced the death of his father, faced his own mortality, and lost a beloved sister. It was therefore a somewhat more mature, if not necessarily wiser, young man who returned to Waseda in the summer of 1922.

Still committed to becoming a writer, Ozaki rededicated himself to his chosen career. Being the head of the family meant that he need not take into consideration what his mother or anyone else thought about his decision. Consequently, from the day he entered Waseda Academy he threw himself diligently into literary activities, which included attending discussion groups and starting coterie magazines (dōjin zasshi). His first important published piece — a story that dealt with the death of his sister Sei — appeared in one such journal in April 1925. Following his year-long sick leave, he graduated from the Academy and, in April 1923, entered Waseda College. At first he considered majoring in English literature, but a professor of Japanese literature persuaded him that students in the English department had to study too hard. He would have no time for writing there, so why not take Japanese literature where the curriculum was far less demanding? That appealed. Ozaki not only wanted time to write but also hoped to pursue his interest in Shiga Naoya, a typical indigenous writer.

His relation with Shiga deepened over the years. In July 1923 one of Ozaki's college friends introduced him to the writer, who from that day became his mentor and 'father figure.' He subsequently visited Shiga many times. Understandably, Ozaki chose to do his graduation thesis on his mentor's works. Despite objections to dealing with a contemporary writer, even though a well-known and established one, Ozaki's persistence and the considerable head start he had made on researching and writing the thesis eventually overcame his adviser's reservations. Gradually, Ozaki went on to become Shiga's most noted follower. Both were committed to writing stories about private experiences by employing a minimum of fictive imagination. Eventually, Ozaki became such an important disciple that he shared with Shiga's heir the responsibility for conducting the famed writer's 1971 funeral and headed the committee commemorating the tenth anniversary of Shiga's passing.

The extent of the inheritance registered in the documents found in the camphor-wood box led Ozaki to believe that there would always be funds available. He acted accordingly, spending 'three to four times the amount that the usual college student needed to live on in Tokyo' in those days. A young man who indulged his friends as much as he indulged himself, he ended up lending money freely. His prodigal generosity brought him some returns, however, when his ability to collect on these loans helped him survive his apprenticeship years as a writer by tiding him over until his work began to sell. The incessant references in early stories to importuning friends for money, or to getting cash from the second-hand bookshop he patronised, accurately reflect his experiences. In an interview, he said that he had no compunction whatsoever about touching his friends for loans because they owed him from college days. And he had provided the owners of the Taikandō with many volumes of considerable value. For literary reasons, however, Ozaki chose to cultivate in his stories the illusion that he was entirely the benefactor of these transactions.

II

Going on twenty-eight and in his last year of college, Ozaki decided to take a wife. He had become involved with Hikida Sumiye (whom he calls 'E' in his stories), a widow who had used the inheritance from her deceased army officer husband to buy a coffee shop near Waseda College. Many teachers and students, including Ozaki, frequented her place. After graduating in March 1927, he moved in with her and immediately plunged into a life of literary activities. Her income meant that he had no worries about shelter or food. Little did he know that in a few short months his own financial resources would evaporate completely.

At that time, Ozaki's relationship with his mother had completely deteriorated. His years at Waseda more or less coincided with a steady split with his family in Shimosoga. As he often reports in his stories, he burned the mail his mother sent him during his final year without ever opening it, and declared egotistically that he would from then on act 'like a villain.' Unknown to him, of course, her letters urged her son to do something about the disaster threatening the family: all the land and property stood in jeopardy of being auctioned off to pay the considerable debts Ozaki had accumulated. As the head of the house, he was in charge of all the family property and consequently it was his responsibility to deal with the problems.

Finally, in July 1927, as Ozaki's mother had feared, financial disaster struck. The effect on the family was dreadful. Expansive generosity and easy ways with money had mortgaged not only his own future but that of his mother, his brothers, and sisters as well. Later, when the banks failed after the 1929 crash, Ozaki forfeited what little property remained. Had a younger cousin of Yatsuka, a retired army officer and headman of a village not far from Shimosoga, not provided funds to buy back the ancestral residence, the family would quite literally not have had a roof over its head.

Straitened financial conditions soon affected Ozaki's relationship with his wife as well. Apparently, Sumiye became tired of supporting somebody whose activities hardly appeared to fit the average person's definition of 'work.' She began to nag him about finding a job and complained that he paid too little attention to her. A man with very definite ideas about how a wife should act towards her husband (she must *depend* on him), he could not easily endure such behaviour.

This was doubtless a turning point in his life. Beset also by the fact that during this period he found himself unable to write and in addition deeply upset by the growing domination of the proletarian authors, Ozaki felt overwhelmed. Uncertain as to how to deal with (and much less solve) the financial, relationship, and artistic problems that confronted him, he decided to turn to his mentor for advice and support. 'I had a single hope,' he writes; 'If I could go to . . . meet and talk with him, I might be able to catch my breath and reorient myself.' Accordingly, he deserted Sumiye in December 1929 and headed for Nara, where Shiga had recently built a new home. As it happened, Shiga was touring Manchuria and did not return to Japan until the end of January 1930. In some stories Ozaki maintains the fiction that his mentor was staying in Onomichi, a quaint port city near Hiroshima, where he had indeed lived briefly between 1912 and 1913.

Removed physically from his various problems, Ozaki hoped to regain perspective and face life once more with greater equanimity. In April 1930 Sumiye visited him in Nara, and tried to convince him to return to Tokyo with her. Ozaki refused. He hoped a fellow writer and mutual friend, Tsubota Katsu, whom he refers to as 'K' in the stories, might marry her and solve his problem. Tsubota had often helped out at Sumiye's coffee shop and, as the altercation between the couple developed, showed more and more sympathy for her. Ozaki similarly felt concerned about her future, but thanks to her business he knew Sumiye would at least have no trouble supporting herself. So after returning to Tokyo in July he severed the relationship. Interestingly, Sumiye appeared to bear him no animosity. During her six-month relationship with Tsubota, for example, she visited Ozaki several times to complain about 'family problems.' After parting with Tsubota she soon acquired a new boyfriend, whom she asked Ozaki to evaluate. He approved of him and the two subsequently married and 'lived happily ever after.'

Meanwhile, Ozaki was a bachelor once again. Though virtually a pauper, at least he had total freedom to practise his craft. The sojourn in Nara with Shiga had provided him with some perspective on life, as well as with a job of sorts. Under his mentor's supervision, he worked on translating into modern Japanese works of the famous Edo story-teller Ihara Saikaku (1642-93), a project Ozaki refers to several times in his early compositions. For a time after he had begun working on Saikaku, he lived with Shirai Hiroshi, a fledgling writer whom he had met at Waseda. Even after moving out of Shirai's flat, Ozaki sometimes visited his friend and his wife, Junko. On one visit he discovered a house guest, Yamahara Matsuye, who had attended school with Junko in Kanazawa. Several months after graduating from her local girls' school in March 1931, Matsuye fell out with her mother and fled to Tokyo. Her naïveté and spontaneity entranced Ozaki, who continued meeting her at the Shirai apartment; after he found himself caring for her, he decided to ask her to live with him.

They rented a room in August and began married life after a 'wedding ceremony' consisting of dinner with the Shirai couple at a cheap restaurant in the neighbourhood.

Although income was a matter of wishful thinking and his future still a question-mark, Ozaki now shouldered the responsibility of supporting a wife. He often had no choice, therefore, but to impose on the friends he had so magnanimously lent money to during his student days. He also managed to suspend pride in his unconventional behaviour long enough to get after-the-fact consent to marry the eighteen-year-old Yamahara Matsuye. The marriage had not, of course, been officially registered, so it could in no way run foul of the law at the hands of some minor bureaucrat in the town hall. At the same time, the civil code formally required parental consent in cases where the woman was under twenty-five. That may have been one reason why Ozaki made the gesture of visiting Matsuye's sister, eighteen years her senior. After her graduation, Nihon Women's College hired Yamahara Tazu to remain at the school as a teacher of Japanese. She also supervised a college dormitory until socialist student activities forced her to move into a flat in Zōshigaya, where Ozaki went to meet her. Fortunately, Tazu happened to be an admirer of Shiga Naoya's work and quite sympathised with Ozaki's interest in writing.

Once Matsuye became pregnant, Ozaki faced another economic crisis: how was he going to pay the doctor's bills? He managed to locate a small hospital with a reputation for being easy on poor people and found a room nearby. In late summer 1932, the couple moved into a six-mat room (9' x 12') in a boarding house down the street from the Kaneda Clinic. The place was gloomy and noisy. People living next door rose early and made a commotion all day long — something that was hardly designed to please a writer who worked at night and slept during the day. Matsuye also had to cope with the fear of the ghosts that she imagined inhabited the cemetery attached to the Buddhist temple just beyond the window. Fortunately, proximity to the clinic made all these inconveniences bearable.

Everything worked out as Ozaki had hoped. Matsuye's stay at the Kaneda Clinic ended up costing very little, and the rest she received benefitted her and her new-born daughter. Combining the Chinese ideographs from their names, *kazu* from Kazuo and *ye* from Matsuye, they christened the girl Kazuye. As one fellow writer exclaimed, 'Well [Ozaki] ... you've come up with at least one masterpiece from amongst all the stuff you've produced.' A number of friends, some, no doubt, indebted from college days, contributed to a cash gift. That plus what he had managed to round up on his own enabled him to rent a small house; at that time, there were plenty of houses available at good prices because the exodus of workers from Tokyo in the wake of the depression had made housing a buyer's market.

Ozaki also solved the problem of finding a dependable yet understanding family physician. He discovered Dr Tsujiyama Yoshimitsu, a man deeply interested in literature and favourably disposed towards aspiring writers; he and his playwright wife made their home a salon for authors. His services were certainly most welcome one day in 1933 when Kazuye, who had suffered from a weak stomach since she was an infant, became violently ill. A childless neighbour lady who loved taking care of the girl had fed her something that did not agree with her and Dr Tsujiyama had to come to the rescue. 'Somehow or other she pulled through, but ever since that time her digestive system was vulnerable and [even at twenty-three] she was still susceptible to colds.' The same doctor also delivered Ozaki's son, Ayu, in January 1935 and gave a speech at Kazuye's wedding in 1957. He was, in short, a close family friend for several decades.

The relative popularity of stories about Yoshibey, one of the names Ozaki uses to describe his wife in his work, kept poverty at bay. He began publishing these stories in the early 1930s, not long after marrying Matsuye. Her irrepressible and eccentric behaviour, naïveté, sincerity, innate goodness, and unconventional attitudes provided all the elements Ozaki needed to fashion a unique female character. As he himself delights in pointing out, there is no other woman like her in all Japanese literature. Of course he garnishes his model here and there to enhance interest in her, adding, for example, many outlandishly absurd statements that Matsuye protests she never made. But even without such additions, there can be no doubt about her uniqueness, or of the general popularity the Yoshibey tales enjoyed; they subsequently won the Fifth Akutagawa Prize for short stories in July 1937. This marked a watershed for Ozaki's writing career and a huge economic boost. Not only did the prize confer ¥500 in cash, enough to pay the rent for nearly two years, the fame attached to the award considerably facilitated the sale of manuscripts to newspapers and magazines. In the years that followed, as he developed a limited though loyal following, Ozaki managed to escape the grinding poverty that had pursued him during the early 1930s.

At the same time that the Yoshibey stories won the Akutagawa Prize, Japan became involved in hostilities with China. As the Japanese people's interest in the war on the continent increased, many literary figures involved themselves in patriotic activities. In the summer of 1940, some ten writers including Ozaki decided to explore a mutual interest in naval affairs, regularly inviting officers from the Imperial Navy to talk to them about the sea. One officer suggested in October that club members experience the ocean directly rather than merely hear or talk about it. Shortly afterwards, Ozaki learned that a group of artists and writers planned to tour Taiwan and South China under the auspices of the Navy to visit naval bases and entertain servicemen, somewhat like a U.S.O. troupe. Forgetting how readily he became sea-sick, Ozaki volunteered to represent his club.

Although the tour lasted only some forty days, it was quite enough to exhaust all the participants. Indeed, one female member — Hasegawa Shigure (b. 1879), playwright, novelist, critic, and editor of a women's magazine — died six months after returning to Japan, presumably exhausted by the taxing schedule. Once back home in February 1941, Ozaki himself had little leisure and not a moment to regain his strength. And later that year, following the outbreak of the Pacific War, the government formally mobilised writers to support the war effort. As a result, Ozaki found himself dashing here and there to give talks at military bases. He also joined a group of writers who edited a patriotic literary journal. By July 1942 he sensed that his varied endeavours were having an ill effect on his health, but there was little he could do to slow down. Responsibility for the January 1944 wedding ceremony of his younger sister, Ei (b. 1908), already in her mid-thirties and long past marrying age, drained him further. The last straw was the mid-summer death, following an operation for stomach ulcers, of his critic friend Aoyanagi Yū (or sometimes Yutaka, b. 1904), 'Y.A.' in the story called 'The Crickets.' Ozaki himself suffered a ruptured stomach ulcer on 30 August, 1944, from which it took a decade or so to recover. Too run down for doctors to operate, he had no choice but to leave Tokyo for his ancestral home in Shimosoga, where he hoped to regain his strength.

Convalescence gave Ozaki considerable time to reflect on his art, his behaviour, his views of life and death. The stories, 'This and That About Bugs' (January 1948) and 'The Skinny Rooster' (January 1949) reveal a man of considerable character trying to survive and, in the process, improve himself and become a better person. The strong moral tone of these stories in a sense symbolises the efforts of the entire Japanese nation to survive a period of adversity, runaway inflation, and a general scarcity of goods, especially food. For Ozaki, personally, the opportunity to evaluate his brush with death forced him to take better care of himself, although apparently he never considered giving up cigarettes or *saké*. One could not guess by looking at or walking with him, however, that he had spent so many years flat on his back suffering such agonies. Even at eighty he could out-walk many far younger than he.

III

Search for meaning, which for Ozaki always implies commitment to authenticity, dominates the three aspects of self-awareness that influence his choice of details. The first of these is self-examination. Here Ozaki addresses the demanding and elusive task of trying to understand experience. To do that, he needed, above all, a relationship. His marriage to Matsuye in 1931 supplied that, as well as a witness to verify his self, as it were, and give direction to his quest for self-identity. She also helped provide the stimulus and opportunities for quiet reflection in his family circle where he could pursue this quest.

There was, additionally, the need to maintain tension between principles and his dreams of being a successful writer. Ozaki's dire poverty provided that tension. For nearly the first decade of his marriage, the pressures of maintaining even a meager existence severely affected his search for meaning and self-discovery. His poverty also constantly put before him the temptation to write what would sell. Because to him writing to appeal to a special readership or to satisfy the whims of an editor violated his artistic integrity, he wrote only what pleased him. And he continued to do so despite the physical suffering this commitment brought him and his family. His principles were severely tried. But he had come to terms with what he felt most important in life: being authentic. So his basic understanding of self and experience compelled him to do what he felt was right. It is not too much to claim that high regard for authenticity and integrity — which reflects his concern for moral problems — runs through all Ozaki's work.

Self-examination of the 'rightness' of his behaviour never occurs, however, as a merely abstract intellectual exercise. Ozaki always searches for meaning in the context of concrete responses to real problems confronted at home. In a number of early stories, for example, he describes how his wife's capricious behaviour provokes his reactions, forcing him to make certain choices and to consider the consequences of his actions. At first he feels embarrassed or shocked, depending on whether he is alone or in the company of friends. And then, again depending on circumstances, he becomes critical or approving; sometimes he takes the view that it may be wisest to leave well enough alone. He becomes more reflective as he ages, but some real domestic tension invariably stimulates his reflections. A 1949 work describes how he imagines he can ferret out the reasons for Matsuye's odd behaviour; his *alter ego*, Ogata Shōkichi, lies 'staring intently at the ceiling ... trying to come up with an explanation [as to why Matsuye had switched off the radio programme he was enjoying]. Unexpectedly, having been given something to think about buoyed him up' as he lay on his sick-bed. Matsuye provides the context for his reflections; Ozaki's concerns to be understood and to understand provide the impetus. Even the way he works out his explanation avoids, in the end, being abstract.

Concrete and personal; real life rather than philosophy. That tells us why Ozaki's search for meaning through self-examination has so little to do with social action. Though the boundaries of his quest remain almost exclusively within the confines of his home, he nevertheless sometimes reacts to indigenous conventions or social problems when they affect him. His remarks on how an old, established family raised its eldest son to inherit patriarchal authority, for example, constitute a scathing if subtle attack on the feudal values of the Japanese family system. And behind what looks like a harmless lament over air pollution in the Tokyo-Yokohama area lurks a stern judgement that shows Ozaki far from insensitive to public problems when they touch him. Absorbing moral concerns induce his reaction; his deeply private nature produces their muted and indirect quality. Even when he wishes to resist the feudalistic family order, which he passionately believes forces individuals to make decisions which aren't authentic, he does so not with head-on rhetoric but by raising his children on a far different model.

To grope for meaning in life by attempting to examine one's self assumes sensitivity to personal motivations, compulsions, and behaviour. Ozaki often achieves greater self-awareness by 'confessing' personal faults, many of which derive from his traditional upbringing as the first son and heir of a proud upper-middle class family. This 'confession,' in turn, allows him to find meaningfulness in the way present behaviour contrasts positively with that of the past. In a word, he tends to use writing as a self-therapist might use a diary: allowing his persona to acquire another mask, the author gains the necessary distance to see his motives more objectively. He also discovers, in the process, how his goals have changed and how he has improved access to 'inner wisdom.' When Ozaki compulsively recites personal quirks or tirelessly points to censurable facets of his personality, particularly when he repeatedly tells how he squandered family resources and lost his patrimony, his revelations contain a tinge of pride that he has overcome youthful character defects. This behaviour then authenticates his integrity as a human being.

Ozaki's quest for meaning through self-examination also saves him from the *de rigeur* modernist pose of being angry at the world

or 'alienated.' Confidence gained in correcting youthful character
faults helps him confront and survive the present. And constant
reflection helps prevent the most virulent sort of alienation, that
from the inner self. Correcting faults and reflection also stimulate a
wholesome sense of perspective. Humour and ability to smile wryly
at his own foibles continually sharpen Ozaki's perspective. In this
way, he charges with positive meaning his reasons for writing about
the self. More than that, his 'confessions' sketch a persona that Ozaki
can fill in or redesign as he struggles to establish his identity and
restore himself to wholeness. The persistent struggle for meaning
restrains personal revelations for sliding into sheer egocentricism.
He may turn inward to explore the motives behind some action or
to puzzle over his wife's behaviour. But the basic drive of his inward
journey — always probing for purpose within a familial domestic
setting that makes it easy for us to identify with the events portrayed
in the narrative — is to find life's meaning, not to vent his anger
over its meaninglessness.

The constant harping on faults, it is interesting to note, is part
of the ambience of a Japanese drinking party, where many intimate
disclosures are said to occur. Though exposed to the ears of non-
family members, revelations made 'under the influence'
conventionally remain private under the fiction that nothing
damaging has been revealed to those not privileged to know. The
pen of the Japanese confessional writer apparently enjoys similar
immunity.

The second dominant concern in Ozaki's stories, desire for
harmony and relationship, rivets our attention on the author's family.
As a young man Ozaki faced the dilemma confronting the first son
of a traditional family, but especially a son who dislikes being bound
by the rules of the system, how to be at once free and related? Close
ties with a 'family' of fellow writers, something that played a far
more important rôle in his life than we can discern from these stories,
compensated somewhat but did not fully satisfy his need for
belonging. Ozaki's struggles to solve this problem had been seriously
complicated by his father's premature death, which placed the duties
and status of the patriarch on the shoulders of a twenty-year old boy
who knew nothing of the world or of the stewardship of resources;
up to that point, he hadn't worked an hour in his life nor earned a
single *sen*. Trying to free himself from the responsibilities while
clinging to the status and the sense of importance the duties of head
of the household gave him only deepened the dilemma — one that
originates in the centrality of relationships in Japan's family-oriented
society.

In Japan it is terribly difficult to acquire a sense of being truly human if one does not belong to some familial group. This suggests the difficulty of being authentic in the sense of having freedom to act according to private principles or the dictates of one's heart. Relationships carry such weight in Japanese culture, in fact, that the individual and his personal values generally become subordinated to the welfare and norms of the group, whether family or nation. It is equally true, however, that relationships, by providing the grounds for meaning and support, allow a person to become what he was meant to be. Looking positively on group identity, any attempt to undermine the structure that functions as a person's primary relationship and ultimate social support is vigorously resisted in Japan. And so any child in Ozaki's milieu who refused to appreciate the sacrifices his parents had made for him justifiably earned social opprobrium as an ingrate who deserved to be a social outcast. This helps explain Ozaki's deep-seated guilt over the way he treated his mother and forfeited the family estate during his twenties.

Guilt feelings exerted a powerful shaping influence on Ozaki's maturation as a human being. Combined with his need for viable inter-personal relationships, which the rift with his mother and siblings enhanced, guilt no doubt contributed to his desire to create a harmonious family circle in which he could learn how to come to terms with those he cared for. Again and again he illuminates his character, enlightening himself and the reader as well, in the process of puzzling over an apparently trivial problem that has arisen at home. As he explores his decisions and the effect they may have on his relationships, he reflects on the tensions between the need for belonging and being authentic. In many stories, therefore, what may often seem a disproportionate amount of 'action' occurs in the author's mind — shunted there by some minor domestic incident, some momentary family tension calling for resolution. Yet he makes the journey inwards, let it be clear, not to escape but to deepen the quality of his relationships. Intuitively he realises that this is the only way he can mature from being a mere individual into a person secure enough to belong without surrendering his principles.

The fact is, we rarely find the hero in any Ozaki story disengaged from reality or from people. And we never observe him wallowing in self-pity or gloating in isolation. When he suffers serious illness and has to be looked after by his family, the Ozaki hero may adamantly maintain an inner life he shares only indirectly by writing a story about it, but nevertheless he does not fail to stress his contact with reality. On the one hand, he thoughtfully responds to his daughter's questions about the nature of the universe and reacts to his wife's antics: but on the other, he is capable of playing a game of patience with a spider caught between sliding windows in the lavatory. On balance, the range of these contacts seems limited. But neither their number nor their quality means as much in themselves as the fact that they demonstrate the author's decision to learn how to live in harmony — a significant condition for sustaining human intercourse in Japan.

Ozaki's wife constantly stimulates or inspires him to live harmoniously, indirectly prodding him into becoming a more caring, a more balanced human being. She binds him to reality, among other things, and in one way or other induces him to learn that immersion in the self alone can neither heal nor enlighten. Strangely, her very unconventionality helps him realise that his quest for meaning and self-mastery must begin with those primary points of contact with the everyday world: his wife, his family. Perhaps a person can only experience the self, as some philosophers claim, but Ozaki implies in practically every short story that solipsism can neither be maintained nor furnish life with meaning. To live meaningfully, one must be related.

Matsuye's very being furnishes Ozaki, or his persona in the stories, constant access to life's small, daily truths, so it matters not at all that she appears indifferent to his quest. She simply enjoys taking on the repetitive and 'meaningless' tasks of the housewife, 'singing a miscellany of school-girl favourites from the late 1920s' as she joyfully attacks 'the laundry that the three children had so diligently managed to pile up daily in the basket.' Her naïveté, spontaneity, and intuitiveness contrast sharply with Ozaki's preoccupation with the nuances of language, his sophistication, self-consciousness, comparative rationality, and concern for authenticity. Contrasts of this sort provide the perspective Ozaki needs to find himself and become whole.

Need for relationship also sheds light on the 'public' dimension of Ozaki's confessional writing. He cannot afford the luxury of imitating Dostoevski's 'underground man,' nor is he by any means the anti-hero who can rely solely on himself for 'salvation.' He clearly needs his wife. He needs his family. Just as a captain needs his ship. That much is obvious. But when Ozaki makes himself an open book, divulging details of family life and domestic intimacies, he symbolically invites others to join his innermost circle. This invitation shows how different his writing is from the typical western confessional. It also creates new relationships for him, bringing into existence an invisible community that expands indefinitely beyond the walls of his home. At that point, the quality of these 'public' relationships often hinges importantly on the author's skill in convincing readers that he is sincere and telling the 'truth.' Whether his stories indeed perfectly duplicate actual life events is less important than whether they create in the reader the feeling that these events must, after all, be what Henry James calls an 'intense illusion of realilty.' Ozaki creates this illusion. His readers accordingly sense that they have a stake in his life, and they grasp with him the significance of the seemingly insignificant incidents and details of family living.

Curiously, Ozaki's 'confessional' technique appears to recreate the sort of relationships occurring in the old-fashioned Japanese bath-house. Stripped of the markers of social status, bathers feel the barriers separating them give way to a sense of family membership. Similarly, stripping away his masks and exposing his relationships, personal problems, and youthful errors to the view of his readers, Ozaki creates a bond that functions as a psychological surrogate for community. The author standing naked in the 'bath-house' of his confessional surrenders privacy and makes himself vulnerable to his reader. Many Japanese, a people who regard vulnerability in others a favourable character trait, feel attracted to the writer so willing to share with utter strangers details about private family relationships and important facts about his inner self.

Thirst for self-improvement, the third dominant concern in these stories, reflects Ozaki's profound interest in character development, in learning how to be ever more true to himself without becoming isolated. Throughout his work we infer a strong desire to overcome faults. And we find him discovering his need to be more honest and more open with himself, which in turn drives him to view himself more objectively, uncover pretensions, and acknowledge limitations. He needs, in other words, what Martin Heidegger calls *Erschlossenheit*, the radical ability to tear down the walls that hem in the self so that one can disclose truthfully his 'existence in the world.' Only by becoming truly naked can a person decide who he will be and then work to become that self. And so it is only after learning to accept his own abilities instead of coveting those of people he admires, and only after seeing the inanity of his pose as a rooster ruling the roost, that Ozaki discovers his mistaken notions about himself. That discovery gives him the strength to see himself as he is and the ability to correct his defects: first steps to authenticity.

Suffering and hardship, experienced acutely by Ozaki during the first two decades of his married life, served as hammer and anvil to reshape his self. First poverty and later critical illness forced him to confront his afflictions with equanimity. Whether he accepted responsibility for his troubles or saw them as predestined, he came to take pride in suffering nobly.

Personal development began the moment he learned to accept,

without passively resigning himself to, the consequences of his acts and the visitations of fate. Only then could adversity temper character. Having chosen to be a writer, he expected a pauper's existence. But physical pain was another matter. He never welcomed it, though his experience with hardship brought on by poverty no doubt made pain somewhat easier to bear. The process of tempering his character began in the midst of poverty with the birth of his first child in 1932. Then his brush with death in 1944, and the years of physical suffering afterwards, truly accelerated his maturation as a human being. The possibility that his family might be left without the breadwinner forced sober contemplation and reevaluation of his attitudes and behaviour. This affected him far more deeply than the start of his family, though that event did goad him to discard certain adolescent poses and begin to act like a responsible husband and father.

Strong belief in the ability to improve character means little without a similarly strong belief in free will. Throughout his stories, Ozaki shows sensitivity to choices and their consequences — that is, he is sensitive to basically moral concerns. He rejects determinism. His decision to be an ordinary husband and father, for example, re-integrates him into the human race, as it were, and makes him aware of some faults. He chooses. He succeeds. He fails. But he remains determined to persevere in the job of making life work. As a result, he becomes a far more reasonable and gentle person, more patient and forebearing with his family. Once he realises the serious consequences his behaviour has for himself and those near him, he rejects all egotistical and self-indulgent defects that encourage poor judgement and cause misery. For Ozaki had consciously committed himself to realising his potential to be a whole and integrated human being without compromising his desire to act authentically.

IV

The stories of Ozaki Kazuo may frustrate those who believe that traditional western solutions to the structure of a novel are inevitable or normative. Had Aristotle read Japanese short stories instead of Greek drama, he certainly would have developed quite different organisational desiderata than he did; and we may not have come to believe that his standards are universal. In truth, whether conventions come from ancient Greece, nineteenth-century England, or modern Japan, rules governing short-story organisation are far from universal matters. They are first culturally-bound and then, within those boundaries, merely fashions. To enhance appreciation of Ozaki's stories, therefore, we must become aware of the cultural conventions and fashions that impinge on his work.

Unfortunately, nowhere in his writing does he explicitly state what his organisational principles are. Claiming, in fact, not to be conscious of such principles, he refuses to discuss them abstractly. This means that we must infer them from the stories themselves. In my view, there are two attitudes in Ozaki's approach to writing which are important influences as regards the organisation of his stories. In the first place, he sees himself and his life as a story — indeed, as *the* story — to be told; this parallels a major Japanese view of the novel, the aesthetic of reality. The second factor concerns the way he considers the story of his life as a series of rhythmic repetitions of certain experiences or events; such repetitions convey a sense of credibility and create large-scale patterns that lend coherence to his work. Understandably, these attitudes may at times reflect some aspect of self-awareness discussed in the previous section.

Ozaki's notion that he himself is the story to be told constitutes the basic orientation of the Japanese private novel, the *shi-shōsetsu* ('I-story'). This genre developed as a loosely organised narrative featuring intimate, confessional details only slightly disguised or fictionalised, and often quite sensational. By contrast, Ozaki never offends the innocent. What he writes may not, however, appeal to those who expect dramatic action. This is especially true when he blends into his story the psychological dimension that earns some of his works the label *shinkyō shōsetsu*, 'stories about the state of the mind.' Whether describing experience or probing his mind, Ozaki believes simply that his life is a story. He no doubt would agree, therefore, with those who insist that the *shi* prefix — the Sinic version of the graph meaning 'I/private' — be pronounced *watakushi*, the usual Japanese word for 'I.' The reasoning is that *watakushi-shōsetsu* more accurately reveals the nature of the genre, for then the sense of the term becomes, *watakushi wa shōsetsu de aru*, 'I am a story.'

Minor artistic omissions, additions, or transformations aside, the *I am a story* approach means writing accurately and naturally about daily experience, about reality. Ozaki does so without imposing superstructures of cause and effect on life's data. The unity of his life becomes the unity of his tale. Of course, this contrasts sharply with the lineal coherence usually expected in western novels. Ozaki's stories offer no rigidly imposed beginning-middle-end schemes. Along with many Japanese writers, he holds that because reality is shapeless no accurate report of it could include nerve-tingling climaxes, neat denouements, and the like. True art means a true copy of life, so Ozaki avoids consciously manufacturing drama or artificially shaping experience. He tries instead to marshal his details so life's recurrent rhythms can create the 'natural' unities and the 'natural' dramas of human existence. One need only slightly rearrange a well-known Shakespearean observation to get at the heart of Ozaki's method: All my life is a story and all the men and women merely characters in it. His 'men and women,' however, are primarily family members. And at times the reflective or contemplative dimension of his subjective novels will reduce the cast of his story to one character: himself.

This is not to imply that these views derive exclusively from Japanese tradition. Far from it. William B. Yeats long ago urged writers who wish to avoid self-deception and insincerity to turn their lives into a play, making themselves and their friends the *dramatis personae*. For Robert Browning, a poem represented the 'effluence' of a man's life and is little more than an abstraction of his person; thus to understand the work one must understand the man. In short, we cannot read a work in complete isolation from the poet's biography. Two modern English novelists take a similar view. Dorothy M. Richardson says she reads books only to penetrate the author's psychology, and Virginia Woolf thought that a book was a person, a real person — perfectly reflecting Walt Whitman's 'this is no book/Who touches on this touches a man.' An 'effluence' of his self, Ozaki can indeed say about his stories, *watakushi wa shōsetsu de aru,* I am a story.

Ozaki's stories are, in fact, so much an 'effluence' of his self that he literally forces the reader to be familiar with his biography. If we are not, we miss the constant allusions to earlier events. If we are, we appreciate the way the author weaves his stories into one seamless cloth by repeatedly including references to the same or some related incident. For example, in late 1959 Ozaki began a serialised story about his youngest child, Keiko (born in 1941), the same Keiko mentioned several times in the present collection. This story features her as a teenager. Once she scolds her father for climbing a ladder to clean out the eaves; though their home is only one story, she believes the task too dangerous for a man of his age. In 1964, Ozaki wrote an essay about climbing the trees in his yard to prune them or harvest their fruit, and there he alludes to this earlier experience with Keiko. He refers to it again in the final story of this collection, likewise published in 1964, in which his wife briefly teases him: 'Things like climbing trees — that's absolutely out of the question, I presume! She assumes that his admission of advancing age will convince him at last to give up this dangerous activity. Note, however, that this brief listing by no means exhausts all references in his writing to tree climbing and aging.

These references lie at the heart of the second attitude affecting

Ozaki's organisational principles: the notion that the story of his life consists of a series of rhythmic repetitions of experience. Quite simply, repeated reference to earlier works constitutes a significant unifying technique. Elements like aging, tree climbing, or relationship — to mention but three — consequently assume greater significance than if Ozaki had mentioned them only once in a single story. Through repetition they become motifs that lend unity to his work. They also require the reader to be familiar with the *oeuvres*, or at least a considerable part of it, if he hopes to appreciate the full significance of isolated allusions. Furthermore, these elements imply that the reality of the author is fugitive and hence impossible to recover from any single story.

This repetitive characteristic of Ozaki's work reflects a well-known feature of classical Japanese poetry: *honkadori*, which means alluding in any individual *waka* to images and ideas in one or more *waka* from an earlier period. A classic poet could neither write nor understand poems unless he had close familiarity with a vast number of *waka*. Each thirty-one syllable work may accordingly share something with previous works in the sense that a single atom shares the structure of the universe even as it contributes to that structure. We might say the same about Ozaki's works. To alter the metaphor, each of his stories participates in a vast mosaic whose repeated patterns and colours create unity in an emotionally satisfying way.

This author's response to events is, moreover, invariably natural. That is, he lets life happen to him and simply reports in a selective manner how he reacts to it. This action-reaction rhythm dominates relationships throughout his work. When Ozaki's wife complains that she has no money for food, he must take action. And he does. Or, the accident of catching a cricket while working in his garden stimulates reminiscences of a war-time experience. That, in turn, reveals much about his special relationship with his younger daughter, and about the background of the serious illness that befell him in August 1944. By not imposing an architectural pattern on these natural events or experiences, Ozaki illustrates his belief that imposed structures create gaps between life and art. Reluctant to create such gaps, he endeavours rather to be 'true' to experience, knowing full well that any description of existence unavoidably becomes clearer and simpler than life itself. But this method, in falsifying reality less drastically than intellectually-conceived structures, permits the author to react naturally to what happens to him. Thus the notion that he only 'harvests' his stories.

Natural reactions to life events seem unconscious. There is, however, a good deal of conscious artistry — without undermining Ozaki's deep commitment to the natural — in other rhythmic repetitions. One such strategy to achieve coherence is constant alternation between his wife's uninhibited and her constrained behaviour. Matsuye (who appears as Yoshiye or Yoshibey in the stories) normally prefers to be her unconstrained self, which means being unpredictable and spontaneous in a milieu where convention reigns supreme.

Rigid expectations as to how a proper middle-class Japanese housewife should behave provide the background against which her totally unbridled naturalness calls all the more attention to itself. On the second visit to a writer friend of Ozaki's (described in the story 'Yoshibey'), she drops all pretense at conventional behaviour. Completely snubbing common sense, she assumes a level of intimacy bordering on the ludicrous. Aside from this example of hilarious behaviour, contrasting so markedly with how conventionally she had deported herself on the first visit, we sometimes see her acting like a scatter-brained dummy and spoiled child or like a serious and responsible wife. Of course, Matsuye had no choice but to become more serious after a ruptured ulcer incapacitated Ozaki in 1944. Her forced switch to responsibility and convention provides the author with endless opportunity to contrast her new ways with the less conventional way she acted before his illness. And to reveal his desire that she return to her unconventional ways.

In another form of the stimulus-response technique, Ozaki unifies disparate experiences by constantly alternating narration with reflection on what his experiences mean. That is to say, he exploits the contemplative and subjective features of the *shinkyō shōsetsu* form. Once again, everyday life at home stimulates him to evaluate thought and behaviour, reflect on life's meaning, or attempt to understand relationships. One day, while convalescing from his bleeding ulcer, he observes some bugs in his room. This, in turn, leads him to consider the meaning of human life. Uncertain of his chances to survive, his thoughtful observations become poignantly moving. On another occasion during his convalescence, Matsuye abruptly enters his room and turns off some music playing on the radio. This forces analysis of her behaviour and gives the author a chance to contrast the 'old' with the 'new' Matsuye. He finds himself thinking that he much prefers the unpredictable woman he had married seventeen or so years earlier. Or, when (in the story 'Putting in For Retirement') his younger daughter chides him for his behaviour on a shopping trip in Tokyo, he feels compelled to reevaluate his attitudes towards and treatment of her. This prompts fresh insights that help him to understand himself better.

Often Ozaki deals with narration/reflection or action/ contemplation by introducing another rhythmic element: alternation between past and present. Flashbacks serve their usual function of providing background details necessary to understand some present problem he wrestles with. Recollection can also restore human qualities, like love and compassion, and give a sense of hopefulness that helps one face life in the present. For example, in 'Day of the Nuptials' Ozaki analyses his relationship with his older daughter Kazuye, whom he feels quite reluctant to see married. He wants to understand his pangs of conscience about her upbringing and why he senses a reluctance to part with her. Reflection, in turn, forces him to consider her babyhood and the extreme poverty that so adversely affected her physical well-being when she was small. All of this resonates with his own character development. By contrast, his present existence is far less severe and he is far more responsible a father. So there is hope for the future, particularly for his second daughter, Keiko.

On another occasion, Ozaki finds himself awakened from a sound sleep by Yoshiye's insistence that he decide what to do with a gold filling she claims had become loose. 'I don't need this anymore. What'll I do with it?' she asks. His immediate response is to reminisce. Musing provides the opportunity to retreat, if only for seconds, into the past. But memories are tinged with shame and assure him only that he had behaved badly, that he is, indeed, 'guilty.' For he failed to provide Matsuye with the 'ordinary comforts' of life, and his poverty had driven him to manoeuver a friend into letting him have several valuable old books. Of course, he desperately needed the money, but he still feels guilty because he had to put his friend on the spot; he also knows he brought his poverty on himself, and that lack of money causes his family a good deal of physical misery. His wife's continued importuning about her loose gold filling bursts the bubble of his reminiscing. By then he feels convinced that he deserves to be aroused from sleep by such a hare-brained question.

The need to purge or rationalise a sense of guilt provides a regular rhythm integrating the *oeuvres:* fall and redemption or guilt and expiation. This rhythm often occurs coincidentally with fluctuations between narration and reflection or during a flashback, as in the above example. Once again, Ozaki's work functions like a diary in self-therapy. Throughout his writing, he almost sacramentally confesses the errors of his youthful ways, especially the insufferable smugness that led him to reject blood ties and bankrupt the family estate. He expiates his sense of guilt first by dwelling on his 'fall' and making a clean breast of purposely having acted, as he often repeats in the stories, 'like a villain.' By alternating descriptions that juxtapose — or at least imply a contrast between — his former and his reformed selves, he asserts his decision to rejoin the human race and redeem himself. As a result, he becomes a more considerate father and husband who also happens to be a hard-working writer dedicated to improving his art. Ozaki steadfastly refuses to accept the idea that man has diminished control over the chaos of daily life! Escaping the penalty of guilt or rejection by admitting past mistakes, incidentally, has long been culturally sanctioned by the Confucian tradition of East Asia, where even modern criminal codes provide lighter sentences for any who willingly come forward and confess.

Expiating guilt brings us full circle to Ozaki's deep commitment to self-improvement, fundamentally a moral concern. Indeed, it is no exaggeration to claim that the dedication to improve himself, a struggle completely indifferent to the passage of time, provides his work with yet another unifying theme. When viewed diachronically, experiences accumulated in the stories verify the author's progress towards this goal. Note also that Ozaki's explorations of this dimension make his life far more available to the reader than had he chosen to indulge in the seamier, sensational aspects of life. As it is, we have little trouble identifying with his desire either to make sense of experience and relationship or to be a better person and writer. His very ingenuousness and forthrightness charm. More important, his writing technique creates pieces that, by inviting the reader to identify with him and participate in his life, break down most artificial barriers between himself and the reader. While lack of artifice makes him more vulnerable, it allows us easier access to his thoughts and feelings. Immediate involvement then facilitates our accepting what we read as the story of a real person in a real family experiencing real problems.

Quite clearly, therefore, the aesthetic behind Ozaki's stories resonates with reality. All three aspects of self-awareness discussed above — whether Ozaki's concern for self-examination, his desire for harmony and positive relationships, or his thirst for self-improvement — reflect the extent to which he roots himself and his aesthetic in reality. The same might be said of his organisational principles. Seeing his life as the story to be told and considering the story itself a series of rhythmic repetitions of everyday experience obviously amount to an aesthetic devoted to reality, or at least to the 'intense illusion of reality' that Henry James believed a work must create in the reader.

If we compress these five elements framing Ozaki's work into a single phrase, we could say that *moral concerns* most characteristically typify his writing, something mentioned consistently in the above discussion. Actually, the moral dimension of Ozaki's stories reflects his struggle for authenticity, his opposition to social norms, his concern to be free from conventions, his resistance to becoming the denatured 'average man,' and his attempts to realise the whole self. In a word, his moral concerns relate significantly to existential themes. And they do so without necessarily negating the indigenous regard for belonging and harmony.

These themes also reflect the basic interest in reality that Ozaki has in common with other Japanese who write in this mode, particularly his mentor, Shiga Naoya. Sharing moral, existential, and realist orientations, these two writers endeavour to depict the search for solutions to the problems of life by writing about the shapeless reality of their lives and welter of personal experience. This is what might be called the aesthetic of reality. On the one hand, the recurrent rhythms of life as they happen in the environment of Ozaki's home — where he must learn to deal with his need to belong, be accepted, and grow — lend structure to his art. On the other, the nuclear family provides every value necessary to give meaning to life and art; it offers, as well, the most natural framework for either. In the process, Ozaki discovers the basic support required to pursue his life effectively as a man and as a writer: existing happily, harmoniously, and authentically in the limited society of his immediate family.

The admiration of many Japanese readers who identify with such a person is surely justified, for the harvest of life's constant flux, stored in his stories, is an abundant crop indeed. In fact, it is far richer than mere descriptions of the miniature world of a single writer in Shimosoga, Japan. And, as I have tried to show, the result goes far beyond being a simple chronicle of 'happy domesticity.' It is, rather, no less than life itself as we know it.

★   ★   ★

Ozaki published the ten stories contained in this volume during a period of more than thirty years. 'Rosy Glasses' appeared in November 1933 and 'Putting in For Retirement' in August 1964. These translations consequently reflect his development as a writer and a human being from the earliest days of his second marriage to his mature period. Only 'This and That About Bugs' ('*Mushi no iroiro*,' 1948) and 'The Skinny Rooster' ('*Yaseta ondori*,' 1949) have been previously published in English. The former appeared in two different versions, one translated by Kumai Hiroo in 1951, the other by William L. Clark in 1958; Edward Seidensticker translated the latter in 1955.

Quite a number of debts have accumulated during the preparation of this volume. First of all, I am grateful to Mr Milton

Rosenthal, formerly of the Division of Cultural Development, UNESCO (Paris), for initially encouraging me to translate Ozaki. I feel similar gratitude to the author, who never failed to respond to my questions, in interviews or in writing, with great courtesy and promptness. But these stories may never have been translated without the generous hospitality provided by the late Mr Iida Kakuyoshi and his widow, Aya, to whom I dedicate this volume. I am equally thankful to their son, Professor Iida Gakuji, for countless hours invested in trying to improve and deepen my comprehension of the text; and, later, for labouriously comparing earlier versions with the Japanese text.

A number of others have also made substantive contributions to the manuscript. Professor Ben Befu not only painstakingly checked drafts of my translations against the originals, he also offered instructive comments on an early version of the Introduction. Dr Donald Brannan and Ms Jan Bardsley also made suggestions on the Introduction that improved the thought development and clarity. Professor Arthur Kimball helped improve the clarity and aptness of the translations. In this respect, I am particularly indebted to the publisher, Mr Paul Norbury, who made countless improvements in the stories; he also went to some trouble to convert my Americanisms into English comprehensible to those in the United Kingdom. Finally, I thank Mitsuko for the thankless job of typing and retyping many drafts through which these pages have gone over the years.

Nine of the ten stories have been translated from the 1968 revised Shinchô Bunko edition of *Nonki Megane* (Rosy Glasses). At Mr Ozaki's request, I deleted the first of the ten stories in that collection, '*Neko*' (Cats), and with his permission substituted '*Mushi no iroiro*' (This and that about Bugs), the seventh story below. This I translated from the 1951 Shinchô Bunko edition of '*Mushi no iroiro*.'

Note that Japanese names always appear in the indigenous order — with surname first.

ROBERT EPP
Van Nuys, California
Summer 1986

1

Rosy Glasses

— 1 —

I heard Yoshiye saying, 'Here, look . . . look at this' . . . and my only thought was, 'Go away!' But this seemingly vague dream would not go away, and the voice finally roused me from a deep sleep. It was morning. Yoshiye was poking something shiny under my nose; my eyes were half shut, my head clouded.

'Look at this,' she was insisting.

'At what?' An oddly-shaped gold-coloured object. I couldn't make out what it was.

'This....Look, it's just broken. It was hurting so I took it out.'

'Oh, it's a gold crown,' I observed, by now completely awake and ready to jump out of bed. But one look at Yoshiye's expression and I thought better of it. Instead, I pulled the bedclothes up to my nose and shut my eyes tightly, unable to utter a word.

I had the feeling that I deserved this. Fair enough, I thought, reflecting on my present situation. I had visions of different faces before me: Mother's. She had told me tearfully, 'Drop dead!' My sister's. She had written, 'Please be the big brother you used to be' ... faces I hadn't seen in all of four years. Then a gentle face, nothing like the sort of face one associates with a teacher's: Yoshiye's older sister. She had told me when I visited her in Zōshigaya a month back to get *ex post facto* consent to our marriage: 'This isn't something for me to approve or disapprove. All I can say is that, since she's the only little sister I have, I'd like you to see to it that she at least has the ordinary comforts.'

'Enough of this!' I thought, suppressing a wry smile. Then another face appeared, that of my friend S. 'Hey,' he said, 'I'm here, too.' About a week ago I went to borrow some money from him again. He said *No* because I'd touched him for money so often. But S's expression changed when I glowered at him. Then, in a controlled voice, he said, 'You're determined not to go home empty handed, aren't you?' Looking triumphant — and at that moment perfectly willing to browbeat him — I replied shamelessly, 'I've no choice.' Momentarily silent, his face pale, S said, 'Well, then, there's no choice.' He got up, slid open the cupboard door with a clatter, and

took two or three ancient volumes in traditional binding from a
wicker basket. Putting them in front of me he said, 'Probably not
enough. But you can do whatever you like with them.' I picked them
up, and placed them in front of me; they were pornographic books
dating from the first half of the nineteenth century. For a while I
lapsed into thought. Then I said, 'Thanks,' my face relatively
composed. But at that moment violent emotions suddenly assaulted
me. My audacious pose melted.

'No matter how humiliated this makes me feel,' I said, 'right
now I have no choice. It's absolutely essential that I get hold of some
money — now. I'd even steal it if need be. There's no way I can
make you understand short of you putting yourself into my shoes.
So swear at me all you want. It won't bother me. I've resigned myself
to that.' I became so distraught that I forgot S was there and,
forgetting my pride as well, let my feelings erupt in tears. I don't
recall how S reacted. But afterwards we played *go* and I left sometime
later . . . .

I heard Yoshiye saying, 'I don't need this anymore. What'll I
do with it?'

Turning towards her I said, 'What do you mean, "What'll I do
with it?"' My best bet in such situations is feigning anger, so I gave
her my scary look and added, 'Why do you do such ridiculous things?
You know we can't afford to get it fixed, and here you go taking
out your crown like that!' She seemed taken aback. But that didn't
stop her from trying to probe my feelings further.

'I'll go and sell it,' she said as though talking to herself. 'And
buy myself some sweets.' I didn't reply. But, in referring to our
wretched poverty, Yoshiye had really touched a raw nerve.

The jewellery shop leaflet folded into last night's paper read:
'Terrific gold boom. X-yen for one *momme* of pure gold; X-yen for
eighteen-carat gold. Now's the time to sell.' I'm sure Yoshiye got
the idea from this advertisement. Her obvious expectation that I'd
be pleased only made me feel worse. Imagining that she wanted to
distract me and lessen the weight of the problems on my mind made
me all the more uncomfortable, since I cannot bear being consoled
by a mere girl of twenty or so. Of course, I suspected that, acting
out of her purely improvident nature and because I was feeling so
low about being broke, she hoped to perk up my spirits. Whether
or not I felt put out, I suppose she did help reduce the tensions ...
so I'd found room in my egotistical frame of mind to take pity on
her. The moment the thought of pity entered my mind, my every
concern focused on her and — in a different sense — I felt
uncomfortable again.

'If you feel better without it,' I said, tempering the look in my

eyes, 'it's all right to take it out. But then what? Since the one on
the other side's still in good shape, don't go taking that one out when
I'm asleep, will you? Or I really will be upset. Understand?'

'Okay,' she said, suddenly beaming. That beam lingered in my
mind as I pulled the covers over my head to get some more sleep.

Around noon I left for our regular pawnshop. I showed the
broker the crown. He said it was eighteen-carat gold weighing 0.7
momme. I got something like four yen for it. The pawnbroker wanted
me to put the money towards the interest we owed him, but I took
it with me and first off bought some food. The incident reminded
me unpleasantly of a funny story I once heard about a fellow who
was completely penniless and, when he had nothing left, pawned
his gold teeth. He bought food with the money, but when he came
to eat the food he had a problem.

— 2 —

Let me summarise the days before I met Yoshiye.

Having no income resulted in dissension with E, to whom I'd
been married for about three years. In addition, my brittle
relationship with mother, still in Shimosoga, had reached the
breaking point. Fed up, I abruptly took off for Nara where a writer
I greatly respect lived in those days. I had one hope: if I could go
to Nara to meet and talk with him, I might be able to catch my
breath and reorient myself. E knew where I'd gone, but they didn't
know in Shimosoga. They found out later when a servant visited E.
But mother resigned herself to my flight. For one thing, once she
realised where I was she apparently more or less assumed what I
had in mind. So she decided not to pursue the matter. I should also
mention that I'm the eldest son in a family where the head of the
house died before his time, obliging me to look after my aging mother
and the three younger children. Mother complained about the way
I handled family finances. Once she called these to my attention, I
acknowledged my mistakes, but she kept badgering me about the
matter. That I didn't like. Actually, I left for Nara with my own
family affairs on the brink of financial disaster.

Once settled in Nara, I could distance my feelings somewhat
from the problems at Shimosoga. After all, I'd done as much as I
could to sort them out. But I still couldn't settle the problems with
my wife. When I went to Nara, I had told my friend K, 'I'm leaving
everything up to you.' I thought as I said it that this was a dirty
trick, but I felt I had no choice. Both my wife and I counted K an
old friend, yet there was a period when we hadn't seen much of each
other because we lived some distance apart. During that time, E and

I began feuding. She said she wanted to go back into the business she had run before. I approved. After returning to where we had previously lived in the city, K often came over to lend a hand. Most of all, my dissension with E astonished him and caused him some concern.

I was inclined to be violent. By then I'd already given up talking to E and I frequently hit her. Once, unaware that her left eardrum had been ruptured, she was shocked to discover dried blood on her ear when she looked into her mirror the next morning. K sympathised with her, and his compassion for her strengthened. After realising that E had already begun to sense K's feelings for her, I no longer hit her so frequently. Our relationship was virtually dead. As I was getting ready to leave for Nara, we exchanged unpleasantries. With a straight face, though in a comic tone, I said, 'When I clear out, you'll have everything your own way, right? Well,' I added with a smile in my voice, 'don't sulk. I'm sheathing my sword.'

'What rubbish,' she said. I didn't bother to note her facial expression when she answered. I was thinking only of what I had asked K to do for me, hoping he would take care of everything.

Obviously, life in Nara allowed me to avoid coming face to face with E. My feelings for her, which had reached breaking point, then relaxed a bit as I had hoped they might. I couldn't help feeling sorry for her. In two or three months my inner turmoil subsided and, after eight months in Nara, I returned to Tokyo and immediately settled accounts with E. She became K's wife and they took a house in the suburbs.

— 3 —

I got to know Yoshiye last summer, a year after my divorce. She had come up to Tokyo from Kanazawa, her first visit to the capital. After a month of seeing each other we in effect became man and wife.

Problems with money had not only forced me to abandon mother and the rest of the family, they also drove me to leave E as well. But more basically, the problem lay in my love for writing stories. Personally, I don't think I'm so clever that the world owes me a living or so stupid that I can't make a living like everybody else. But I grew more and more enamoured of writing. By the time I realised that the inheritance from father had evaporated, it was too late: I had utterly squandered the basic resources to get through life. Because I had no interest in such things even when financially solvent, I ended up empty-handed in every sense of the term — a homeless cur lacking the vitality to run, even if shooed away. That's just about what I was, too. Following my divorce, I was content to be alone.

All along, I'd never imagined I could write anything that might truly please me. But I had also from the outset resigned myself to the realisation that I had no hope of making a decent living — even if I could please myself. So I felt carefree because any hardships would be mine alone. Believing that I was stuck with the old wife and that I'd never remarry allowed me to concentrate on writing. Indeed, my trip to Nara had encouraged me to think that I could get back to it again.

When I became interested in Yoshiye and learned that she was interested in me, I naturally hesitated. But I took the plunge and got married. I was overwhelmed by the beauty of her feelings, so uncomplicated and child-like. On the other hand, I couldn't help worrying about whether I might be cruel to this woman, too. My worries only intensified when I thought of her as a young, happy-go-lucky girl ignorant of the world.

— 4 —

We are renting a shabby six-mat room in a private house. In our nine-by-twelve home we have a desk, a bookcase, and an empty chest of drawers lined up against one wall. We do our own cooking on a portable stove set up in a corner of the hallway. The landlord apparently doesn't put much store in my saying I'll pay for everything just as soon as I finish my work, so he declines to continue providing meals. We've accumulated quite a bill for our lodgings here. I'm somewhat upset by the fact that he refuses to give me breathing space and let me do my work in peace, since at the moment I'm not exactly sitting around doing nothing. He stopped serving meals when we couldn't come up with even a small part of what we owed. So I told him that running around here and there to get something to eat each day only puts me further behind schedule. 'Won't that disadvantage both of us?' I asked. He simply ignored my argument, saying, 'We're hard-pressed too.' What with the exasperation and the running around, my work makes little headway. I'm clearly aware, too, that since I'm working on one volume of a series the further behind I get the more I stand to lose.

— 5 —

Yoshiye's comparatively happy-go-lucky attitude in the face of our harsh existence makes it easier for me. At the same time, however, I feel constantly under pressure. I wonder how long her devil-may-care attitude will last. A rubber band can stretch only so far. I keep thinking I'll have to do something before it snaps. Feeling restless,

I nevertheless maintain a nonchalant expression with happy-go-lucky Yoshiye sitting next to me jabbering along in her happy-go-lucky way.

She particularly loves talking about her childhood. It depresses me to imagine that her present misery drives her to return unconsciously to the happier times of the past. What she talks about is totally inane. In most cases I only respond perfunctorily, not listening to a thing she says. Still ...

When she was five, a turkey ran after her because she had on a red kimono; since then she has referred to it as her 'turkey rags.' Out to pick some flowers, she fell into the river and a passing postman saved her; that kimono became her 'river rags.' She had heard time and again from her mother that when the famous eighteenth-century scholar, Arai Hakuseki, was three he wrote the Chinese graphs for *tenkaichi*, 'world's best,' with great skill on a folding screen. But when she wrote *tenkaichi* in huge characters on a freshly-papered sliding door she stunned her mother. She was six.

The following year she lost her father. 'He'd be seventy if he were still alive. I remember him as an old man who played *go*, practised calligraphy on paper laid over a red cloth, drank *saké* at night, and — with his skinny legs — looked like he was sinking into the mats. He also had a funny habit —' Despite having two lavatories, one indoors and one outside, her father urinated in a bucket he kept in the yard. When she was about four, Yoshiye habitually followed him to take a peek. Her father scolded her and sent her back into the house. The bubbles constantly floating in the bucket fascinated her. 'It's quite true, father used it for fertiliser. He'd planted just a very few eggplants and cucumbers in one corner of the yard. Sad excuses for vegetables — you could count on your fingers the number that came up. He said the fertiliser had to be his own pee. Anyone else's was unsanitary.' Yoshiye nearly split her sides with laughter over her father's strange antics. It amused me to watch her break out laughing at her own stories. I let her chat go in one ear and out the other, preoccupied with my own thoughts as I dredged up incidents like the following.

— 6 —

Some two months back we fled these lodgings after the landlord suddenly pressed hard for payment. Telling Yoshiye I was going out to raise some money, I got up to leave. But she grabbed me and wouldn't let go. She started crying about how she hated staying in that room alone. I took her along. Actually, from the outset I had little hope that I could scrape up even a pittance that day. Soon it was dark. Like a horse that balked at pulling a cart, Yoshiye wouldn't hear of going back to our room. I took her to a friend's place.

I went up alone. My penniless young friend, Shimizu, lived in a seedy third-floor room of about eighty square feet, a mere four-and-a-half mats. I got him out of bed. 'Hi!' he said. I told him I'd like to stay the night.

'Fine. And Yoshiye?'

'She's downstairs by the entrance. Could you put her up too?'

'Sure. So you finally gave them the slip, eh?'

'Looks like it, but we haven't brought a thing with us. We hadn't planned on leaving.'

'You'll go back tomorrow and nonchalantly sneak a little something out, right? Well, I'll go down and borrow some bedding.'

'Look, on your way down how about telling Yoshiye to come on up?'

'Fine,' he said, heading downstairs. But when Shimizu returned a few minutes later, an odd expression on his face, he told me that Yoshiye wasn't there. I couldn't imagine what on earth had happened. I said nothing; then he asked, somewhat concerned, 'Shall we go and look for her?' I remembered that Yoshiye had been quite agitated, so I became a bit concerned too. But at the same time, however, I was seething inside.

'Well,' I said, 'she'll be back soon. She's got nowhere else to go ...' I stood thinking for a while, then went over to the window and shouted into the midnight darkness: 'Yoshibey! Hurry it up — or else!' And I added with some vehemence: 'Nitwit!' No answer. I heard only the echo of my *nitwit* bouncing off the bunkhouse of the college baseball team on the other side of the empty field facing the flat. I could tell my face was livid with fury.

'But she's got nowhere else to go,' Shimizu insisted, 'so ...'

'To hell with it. All this concern might spoil her. If she doesn't come back pretty soon, that's it. Meantime, let's get some sleep.'

'Shall we?' Shimizu laid out Yoshiye's bedding. That made me all the more annoyed with her.

About half an hour later I heard someone coming up the stairs. I knew it was Yoshiye. The sound of her long strides stopped outside the sliding doors. Then that devil-may-care voice: 'Hi, there!'

'Come on in,' Shimizu answered, getting out of bed.

'Where the devil did you gallavant off to anyway?' I said, trying to quash my deep feelings of relief. 'You daft thing!'

'Oh,' she groaned, rattling the *shōji* door with her foot. 'Open up.'

Shimizu opened the door.

'Hi! Gosh, this is heavy,' she said, dropping the *furoshiki* bundle on the floor.

'What's that?'

'Our kimonos, bed clothes, pillow cases, blankets, and things,' she said as she set about undoing the knots in the *furoshiki*.

'What on earth!' I glanced at Shimzu who had just turned towards me, his eyes wide with astonishment. 'Wow!' he rasped. Then he looked at me: 'What do you think of that?'

Touched, I said with a smile, 'She's happy-to-lucky, that's all ... Okay, no scolding. You're just in time with all this.'

'Shouldn't I have brought it? But your friend doesn't have any of these things. No extras anyway.'

'No, it's great you brought it all. Bet it weighs a ton.'

'I didn't mind the weight. But it's the middle of the night and I was scared stiff all the way over here.'

'Well, let's get some sleep. This has been a tiring day.' I was the first to lie down. Yoshiye set about sorting out the contents of her bundle: this for Shimizu, this for you, this for me. Immediately afterwards she got ready for bed. Soon she stretched out and before long began snoring.

I stared silently at the ceiling. Weary as I was, I couldn't sleep. I was just thinking that Shimizu, likewise on his back with his eyes shut, might be in the same fix when he said without moving, 'Well, you told me again and again, "She's happy-go-lucky, I mean happy-go-lucky" ...'

'Still,' I said, 'that doesn't quite explain all of her. But she is an optimistic, uncomplicated rascal, that's for sure. That's precisely why, for my money, I'm all the more ... what shall I say ... ?'

'She's young, too ... Listen, I'd like to see you polish off this job. That's your number one priority right now.'

'I know. The problem is, I end up frustrated these days ... I feel as though I'm constantly being outmanoeuvered. You know, like in a game of *gō* or *shōgi*. If only I could take the initiative ... '

'I know what you mean.'

Soon Shimizu dropped off to sleep too.

*   *   *

Two or three days later the room next door was vacated. We decided to rent it, bedding included, and moved in.

The field across from our third-floor windows was divided into three areas. The section on the side with the baseball bunkhouse was just a vacant lot serving as a small field for the college players and neighbourhood children. A tennis court and miniature golf course occupied the sections facing the art school. Sitting in Shimizu's room, once we watched two college students playing catch on the field. Noticing us, one raised his arm and waved his glove; apparently he recognised Shimizu.

'He's asking us if we want to play,' Shimizu said. 'How about it? I've got the gloves.' He was ready to get up so I decided to go. Yoshiye tagged along.

Since I hadn't touched a baseball for a decade, I made up my mind to go for the catcher's mitt because I didn't want to end up with a sore shoulder from throwing the ball too hard. I'd frequently hurt myself merely playing catch, however, so even with the catcher's mitt I was timid and didn't go to meet the ball. I was always fumbling or letting it zip by me.

Yoshiye, who had been watching us play, called out in her native dialect: 'Butter-butter-butterfingers. I canna' bear a watchin'!'

'Don't be so cocky. Try it yourself and you'll soon find it isn't that easy.'

She claimed she could do it, so as a joke I handed her my glove. She started putting it on her right hand but caught herself and switched to the left. Then she turned to us, ready to play. Chuckling, neither of us took her seriously. Still, when Shimizu tossed a ball to test her out she caught it properly. It was no rubber ball, either, but a regular hard baseball. I put on a glove and threw her two or three balls.

'No kidding,' Shimizu said with a straight face, 'she's better than you.'

'She's something all right,' I said, about to make the same conclusion. 'Hey,' I asked Yoshiye, 'have you ever played this before?' She said she'd never played baseball at school, though she had been on the basketball team. I was a bit relieved to hear that. Then I tried throwing the balls harder and harder. When that didn't worry her, I said the next one would be a burner. I really put my weight behind it but she caught that one, too. In fact she hardly dropped any.

Then I remembered that Yoshiye was pregnant. Damn! I thought. I insisted she stop then and there and told her to go up to the room and rest. She didn't look too happy about going. Unobstrusively I gave my tummy a pat. She put her hand to her head, *oh no!*, and went straight to our room.

Shimizu and I soon followed her. He began talking about nothing in particular. I simply said, 'We goofed. She's a little too easy going.'

From the tone of my voice he realised that something was up. He became serious and asked, 'What do you mean?' Yoshiye made a peculiar face when she saw my cantankerous glance.

'She's expecting.'

'Oh, so that's it? Well, then . . .' Not knowing whether to offer congratulations or condolences, he hesitated momentarily before saying, 'I hope she'll be all right.'

'Looks like this is exactly the time she's supposed to be careful. She recently read something to that effect and we'd just been talking about it. I let it slip my mind, too, but most of all it's up to her to watch it. No more playing around as a tomboy, is that clear?'

'Okay.' She looked unhappy.

That night Yoshiye dropped off straight away as usual, but I simply couldn't get to sleep. Since I kept hearing Shimizu turning pages or something, I went next door after a while to see him.

He lit up a cigarette and chuckled as he inhaled deeply. Exhaling he said, 'She really put on a show today, didn't she?'

'Quite a show. She certainly is an odd one,' I said. It tickled me, too, and I couldn't stop smiling. '"Blind men dont't fear snakes" — that's her,' I said, thinking of the ball-catching episode. I thought again how she's like that in almost everything. It's a bit awkward writing about such things, but you can say the same thing about how Yoshiye got pregnant. I had told her that getting in the family way at this point would be a headache. Consequently, we should use some birth control device until our situation improved. I got her to agree to use a particular device, though her consent was not wholehearted. Nor did I realise at first that she had cunningly rendered the device useless. Later, I became suspicious and, when I checked to make sure, she apologised tearfully saying she so much wanted a baby. I reflected on that a while before saying, in what for me was a gentle tone, 'I understand so it's okay. Don't cry. We won't be using birth control anymore. Just have a terrific baby, all right?' Yoshiye nodded vigorously, still snivelling. I patted her shoulder.

This is not something I can very well mention to others. Nor did I feel like telling Shimizu. All I told him was, 'We're too badly off to have kids.'

'Well,' he said, 'you have no choice now.'

'Or rather,' I said, 'from Yoshiye's viewpoint it was foolhardy to take up with a fellow like me in the first place.'

'The particulars of your marriage aside,' Shimizu beamed, 'from an outsider's view I suppose that's what it amounts to. But some of us wouldn't know what to do if it weren't for foolhardy people or oddballs. Just imagine how it would be if we had no life partner to look after us. Obviously, though, that's another problem.'

'Right. Another problem.' Sensing that our conversation had lost its point, I said no more. After a while I returned to my room and fell asleep.

Late one afternoon two or three days later, I ran into an

acquaintance on the street. It was Kumihama Shinaye, a newspaper reporter's wife — a woman who ran a model agency and who enjoyed gadding about all day busy as a bee.

'Hi there!' she said in her characteristically masculine way.

'Hi there! What a surprise.'

'Hardly a surprise,' she said. 'I've been looking for you for some time. Where on earth are you guys holed up these days? ... Say, let's stop in over there for a breather. We can't talk on the street.'

We went to a nearby teahouse. Shinaye asked whether she could use Yoshiye as a model. The basic requirement of any model is good looks so, not thinking that my wife had the qualifications, I shrank from Shinaye's enthusiastic proposal.

'As far as I'm concerned,' I said, 'since I can't resist the money I have no objections. But ... well, do you really think she's suitable?'

'Oh, there's nothing to worry about! Just dab a little here, smooth out a little there ... I can use her quite well.'

'You really think so ... ?'

We talked about it but in the end it came to whether Yoshiye herself might be interested. With that I decided to run my errands and have Shinaye talk to her alone.

By the time I got home some three hours later it was already dark. I found Yoshiye sitting idly in our room.

'Did Shinaye stop by?'

'Yes.'

'Well, did you take it?'

'I said no. But you see she was so persistent. And besides I'm interested in the money, so ...'

'Do it if you can. I'm a bit concerned about your condition, though ... do you think she noticed it?' I asked, pointing to my stomach.

'Not really. I'm still rather small so nobody's aware of it yet. She says I should relax and it'll be as easy as winking.'

'Really? Well, then, go ahead and take it easy. Now, that'll be an experience for you!'

'I'll do it, but I'll feel self-conscious. That's for sure.'

'What are you talking about? Just think of all those people as pebbles or puppets.'

'Shinaye told me the same thing,' Yoshiye said, breaking into laughter. 'Look how much she gave me,' she added, showing me the money.

Apparently, Yoshiye's own kimono would be more or less adequate, so Shinaye had left the money as an advance so we could redeem the garment from the pawnshop. The job, concerned with public relations for a *saké* firm, would run for a week beginning the next day at the Shirokiya Department Store in Nihonbashi.

The next morning Yoshiye managed to put up her hair, apply her make-up, and get her kimono out of hock. But putting on her *obi* threw her for a loss. What with only a single hand mirror, and because she had no one to assist her but me, she couldn't get it right. No matter how much she tinkered with it, the bow in the back looked odd, even to me. It was frustrating, but I wasn't about to throw up my hands in despair. Finally, I patted one indifferent-looking bow and said, 'This one's fine. It really looks great.' Arms behind her, Yoshiye momentarily ran her hands over the bow. Then she burst into tears. 'I'm not going.' The tears could spoil her make-up, so I said all sorts of things to try and calm her down. Then I imposed on the landlady, busy as she was, to redo the *obi*. It was already past nine-thirty, however, and Yoshiye was supposed to be at Shirokiya's by ten.

As we stood on the curb to flag down a cab, passers-by gave us the once-over. In view of the fact that she was decked out so smartly and made up heavily, and because it was still early morning, I suppose it was natural for people to gawk. But when one chap who passed by made some comment I scowled at him. Yoshiye looked to me like a tall and stately woman — but a total stranger. When the cab passed Gofukubashi and we could see Shirokiya's ahead, I repeated the usual reminders. We got off at the Nihonbashi intersection.

'Stay calm, now, Yoshibey — okay?' I said it earnestly. 'They're all pebbles and puppets.' Apparently, I must have spoken a bit loud because people nearby looked in our direction. But I paid no attention. Yoshiye nodded her *takashimada* coiffure ponderously and flashed a smile. Then she abruptly assumed a prissy expression, the likes of which I had never seen, and crossed the tram-car tracks. I studied carefully the composed way in which her tall, well-knit frame glided across the street. At that moment, for some strange reason, I felt a glow of warmth and compassion for Yoshiye well up within me; strangely, I seemed to be savouring it — shamelessly. Nor did I feel the slightest desire to hide my emotions as I walked crestfallen to the stop for the Waseda-bound tram.

Yoshiye worked seven days without a hitch. We returned to our old lodgings with at least a little pocket money . . .

— 7 —

Slouched over my desk, I noticed vaguely through half-closed eyes that Yoshiye had slumped down on the mats. She had decided that our baby would be a girl, so she was thinking constantly about nice feminine names and pink clothing. She's a strange one, all right.

'Sleepy?' Yoshiye asked me.

'Hardly,' I said, sitting up straight. 'Say, you're the one that looks sleepy.'

'Not me. But you're not listening to me. It's not fair to let me talk on and on like that.'

'No, I'm listening as well,' I said. 'I was just thinking about something else at the same time.'

'Like what?'

'Like a blindman fearless of snakes.'

'How ghastly, I detest snakes.'

Yet she never gives that impression, I thought, smiling to myself. If she ever opens her eyes . . . well, even Yoshiye's thick 'rosy glasses' can't help getting broken some day. How will she manage then . . . ?

'Ooh, I've had it,' she sighed leaning back, both hands on the mat.

'You're probably worn out from all that chattering.'

'I suppose so. Actually, I'm a bit sleepy, too.' She sat up properly and rubbed her eyes. And then — whatever could she have been thinking? — with a flick she turned her eyelids inside out and leaned toward me.

'Can you do this?'

'Damn! What's that supposed to be? Don't do that.'

'I'm not much good at it anymore,' she said, getting her eyelids back to normal with a blink. The stunt had filled her eyes with tears.

'You know, whenever the doctor checked us at school, I flipped my eyelids like this. Every single time. We'd line up in order, you know. My turn would come and when the doctor raised his hands to check my eyes he'd find my eyelids already flipped up. "Goodness — for crying out loud!" he'd say. Every single time . . . But if I don't keep at it I can't do it smoothly. Naturally, it's a matter of practice.'

'I imagine it is,' I answered, slightly unnerved.

— 8 —

I had little trouble getting started on 'Rosy Glasses' once I got the idea to write it. About half way through, however, my pen ground to a halt. I put the story aside for a while, but when I tried to tackle it again I was even less able to warm to the task. My focus had blurred. Little by little my heroine's happy-go-lucky nature had begun to erode. In everyday life terms, this necessarily also affected the man in the story, the narrator. I repented not having written it out at one sitting, but by then there was nothing at all I could do

about it. Trying my utmost to recreate the atmosphere in which I
had originally begun to write this piece, I'm attempting to finish it
up now. As you may well imagine, however, I'm far from satisfied
with the results.

★   ★   ★

I find that I have unconsciously closed my eyes to the facts. The
uncertainty of how much longer Yoshiye's happy-go-lucky attitude
might last weighs on my mind with increasing heaviness. This forces
me to face up to the realities of my situation. Yoshiye has already
become depressed. It's not that she has said anything specific, but
I once happened to see some ugly lines chiselled into the corners of
her eyes.

One quiet evening she unexpectedly came up with the following.

'Darling . . .'

'What?'

'You know . . . people, . . .'

'Let's hear it, then, come to the point!' Being an impatient
individual, I detest beating around the bush.

'You know . . . people . . .' Then she rattled off what was on
her mind: 'When people die, that's the end, right?'

'I suppose so,' I said. 'Why do you ask?'

'Does that include pain and grief, too?'

'Of course. "In the beginning there was neither East nor West,
how can there be North or South?"'

'What on earth is that, something from *mahjong?*'

'Certainly ...'

'Come on,' she said. 'I'm serious. You're teasing me.'

'When you die, that's the end.'

'Really? Well, that's a load off my mind. What a relief.' Yoshiye
actually did seem relieved. I was somewhat bewildered.

'But it's not something you can dispose of so neatly,' I said.

'Why not?'

'Well . . . oh, forget it. You're better off not thinking about
such things.'

'As long as I know that death is the end, I don't need to think
about it.'

What rotten luck for Yoshiye! She'd grown up carefree, and
then at eighteen drifted to Tokyo where almost immediately she
became involved with the likes of me. I had told her, 'No matter
how rough life gets, if you think it's a joke, it's a joke, okay? There's
nothing to it. Come what may.' I myself had by no means been
putting on a false front. My father's death, the death of the elder of

my little sisters, my own serious illness, the Kanto earthquake, the
failure of the banks — over the four years before I turned twenty-five,
this succession of disasters had dulled my senses. Nothing frightened
me any longer. But I had begun to avoid trouble more than ever.
For that reason, always expecting the worst, I'd assumed a 'who
cares?' attitude. I would sit around taking no definite action but
simply wait for whatever woes might come. This attitude helped me
weather with comparative ease, considering the gravity of the
problems, both the quarrels with my family and the break-up with
my former wife. That's the sort of person I am. But when I think
of Yoshiye, who has nobody to depend on but me and who never
grumbles about her harsh existence, it's depressing — even for me.
When it comes to someone who carps at me, I can say nearly anything
straight to his face. Once I told my mother, 'From now on I'll be a
villain.' But I could never say that to somebody helpless and docile.

My passion for writing and the tension which that passion
generates in me are all that hold body and soul together. All my
ambitions centre on writing. Of course, realising I'm no more than
a 'heated-up stone' demoralises me. But if I were stripped of my
ambitions, only something resembling a jellyfish would remain. My
eyes would dim, my back would become stooped, and I would lose
my appetite. So, lacking talent, my ambitions simply spin around
and get nowhere. And yet they are all that sustain me. I may say,
'Bread before Art,' but the fact is that such statements simply do
not reflect my reality. From time to time I've thought, 'This won't
do!' But at the moment, I'm reduced to a situation where I have no
choice. Literally, I'm a critically ill patient on whom the doctors
have given up hope. Like medicine that has lost its efficacy, I no
longer respond to admonitions: 'Turn over a new leaf!' or, 'Pull
yourself together!' Ultimately, I've no choice but to continue as I
am. Some positive good may come from ascertaining what happens
to somebody who has elected to take such a path in life, however
much in error it may be.

Once, with an unusually serious expression on my face, I said,
'Yoshibey, this must really be miserable for you.'

'Do you really think so, darling?'

'I do.'

'If you do,' she said beaming, 'that's fine. Your thinking, so it
is enough to make me happy.'

Can you imagine tormenting a person like her? Ohhh! I groaned
to myself. Was it worth subjecting her, I wondered, to all this simply
so I could write a story? On the heels of that thought there sprang
into my mind, like a reflex, the idea that, yes, there is no other path
for me. So perhaps the one who's been wearing 'rosy glasses' isn't

Yoshiye at all. Maybe it's been me. Certainly it's possible to look at it that way . . . but unfortunately, such rosy glasses are not likely to break for a whole lifetime. That elicits a faint smile.

(November 1933)

2
Yoshibey — On Conventions

Yoshibey — that's my wife. Her proper name is Yoshiye; age: twenty-two; height: five-feet two; weight: 116 pounds. So, in the first place, she's larger than the average woman. Yet despite her size she's an incredibly nervy person. She's not only highly strung but, as far as I can see, quite devoid of common-sense. In the presence of strangers, for example, she blurts out things better left unsaid. Or, if displeased with something, she literally pouts right in front of people. And when she's ecstatic about something, her beaming face broadcasts exactly what she feels. I don't particularly like calling such a scatter-brained tom-boy 'Yoshiye' in front of others. So I call her 'Yoshibey'- a boy's name.

* * *

One evening Yoshiye said: 'Do you know why I hate going into the kitchen at night? I'll tell you. It's the cord on the skylight. It dangles in a loop like a hangman's noose. What if my neck got caught in it?' She clutched her neck with both hands. 'Aaaagh!'

Ridiculous? Maybe, but one cannot dismiss it quite so simply. Such an attitude is foreign to my sensibilities, although it does make some kind of sense.

On another evening I was coming down from the second floor when Yoshiye, hiding round the corner at the bottom of the stairs, suddenly jumped out and yelled, 'Boo!' When I replied coolly, 'Did you want something?' she froze in front of me, aghast.

'What are you up to anyhow? Funny idea of a joke.'

'You scared me. So I thought I'd scare you back but I only scared myself. Look how I'm sweating.'

'Just don't go on doing that sort of thing. There really is a limit to your idea of fun.'

Was she shocked by my calm or had she been rattled by her own voice? Or maybe this is what happened. She stands holding her breath in the hushed semi-darkness; someone comes along who doesn't expect her to be there; an odd scream breaks the quiet. It's

her voice, but she can't imagine it belongs to her, nor can she be
sure whether she is that someone, or that someone is she. This,
however, remains only my personal view, and I don't imagine that
it can explain Yoshiye's phobias. Every time I ask she just repeats
the same answer: 'I haven't the faintest idea why, I'm just scared.'
In a word, I haven't a clue how she feels on such occasions. Though
I've devoted some thought to it, I have yet to come up with the
answer.

'At any rate,' I said, genuinely upset as I plopped down by the
hibachi, 'it's stupid to try to startle somebody and end up by startling
yourself.' I'm sure I looked utterly nonplussed. Yoshiye seemed
ready to cry.

'You're mean.'

'Don't give me that,' I said glaring at her.

'But I was really scared,' she whimpered.

By then I was quite irritated, but I didn't let myself get too
upset. Reluctantly, I said with all the calm I could muster, 'You're
not very convincing, you know.' Of course I didn't imagine for a
moment that Yoshiye would understand what I was talking about.

★   ★   ★

On another occasion — this time in broad daylight — she suggested
stopping the clock because its tick-tocking was so scary she couldn't
stand it. I was at my desk, vacantly puffing on a cigarette. I snuffed
it out, tossed the butt into the *hibachi*, and turned around.

'Yoshiye, come here!' I rarely called her by her proper name.

She came in dragging the knitting she had been working on,
the ball of yarn unwinding behind her.

'Sit down.'

'What is it?' She sat down and was about to start her knitting
again.

'Stop that!'

'But I've got to get it done for the baby. Didn't you tell me to
hurry up and finish it?'

'Now, no more of your nonsense. Just listen, is that clear?
Clocks are made to tell the time. They're constructed in such a way
that they make those noises.'

'Oh gosh, I know that.'

'Shut up! There's nothing mysterious in the fact that they go
tick-tock because they've been built to make such noises. So what's
there to be afraid of? You ... you're always saying, "I'm scared, I'm
scared," but half the time it's rubbish. You're making it up, aren't
you? You just enjoy pulling my leg, saying anything that comes into

your head. Isn't that right?'

'I don't mean to pull your leg,' she said, a bit deflated.

'You're sure? If that's rubbish, too, you'll be sorry. Is that clear?'
Yoshiye nodded.

'But if you really are afraid ... well, then, we've got a real
problem. What on earth's the matter with you anyhow?'

'That clock always tick-tocks, but it's never bothered me before.
I'll be in the middle of doing some knitting, you know, then all of
a sudden I can't get the sound out of my head. It keeps ringing in
my ears. On and on. Little by little a strange feeling comes over me.
Finally, I really begin to feel scared.'

'The reason it ticks, silly, is because it's wound up, and since
we wind it whenever it runs down, it'll always tick. We often say
that steadiness is the characteristic of machines, but a clock that isn't
steady would not be much of a clock. You're going to be terrified
of anything and everything when you're obsessed with thoughts like
that.'

'I suppose you're right. What you said about clocks — I know
that. But I don't think about that when I get scared. I'm just scared.'

'That's the problem. Now, in future, whenever you imagine
you're scared, put your foot down there and then. Try to think
things out. "This is what's happening; I should expect this; it's not
the least bit strange." See what I mean? Remember the time your
sash got caught in the sliding doors and you were really agitated
saying somebody was tugging at you? You should have stopped to
think about it for a minute: "There's no reason for anybody to be
tugging at my sash." Right? You had just washed your hands after
going to the toilet; you closed the door to the hallway, opened the
shōji door to our room and came in. It's impossible that somebody
could have been tugging at your sash from behind. Shouldn't you
have tried then to think of a few alternative explanations — for
example, that your *kimono* or whatever might have snagged a nail
or got jammed between the *shōji?* Whenever you think something
strange is happening, make a point of considering whether or not
it's even possible.'

'But whenever it happens I can't think. That's just the way I am.'

'Well, it's damn annoying.'

My admonitions had lost their original impact so I left it at that.
I sent Yoshiye back to the living room and, propping my chin on
the desk, soon became lost in my own thoughts.

The old worry about what if Yoshiye were sick returned. But
however I looked at it, I couldn't imagine her being sick. She slept
well, ate well, worked hard, her complexion was good, she weighed
enough, she produced lots of milk for the baby. Perhaps there are

instances when a person's nerves might break down independently of the body, but I could never face up to the worries of such a possibility.

I'm not exactly sure when it was, but Yoshiye had finished washing her hair and was doing something in the kitchen. Nearly dry, her hair fell over one shoulder and down her front. As she stooped over to pick something up, her hair touched the gas burner and caught fire. Since I was just about to tell her to watch out, I dashed from the living room to put it out. I could hear the crackle of the flames which had taken hold. I rubbed her hair between my hands to quench the fire. Both my palms were covered with bits of burnt hair and I had broken out in a cold sweat. By contrast, Yoshiye was shrieking with laughter.

'Even before I knew what the crackle was, you were flying towards me, a horrified look in your eyes. It was really a scream!'

My kind of fear apparently didn't register. Hers was simply the sort that bypasses reason; one might even call it a primitive fear. She was not particularly afraid of what she did not feel.

★   ★   ★

The following episode illustrates what I mean by Yoshiye's muddle-headedness.

F is one of my comparatively recent friends. He stopped by the house for the first time when I was out.

'May I ask your name, sir?'

'Do you have a message I might pass on to my husband?'

'You've been kind to stop by; would you care for some tea?'

From what F told me later, Yoshiye had received him with every courtesy. She had knelt properly on the mats and had even arranged her fingers nicely when she bowed. F said that there was scarcely any similarity between that Yoshiye and the one he'd imagined from reports and from reading my stories. He said he was so bewildered and bewitched by her politeness that he found himself bowing again and again in extreme deference when he left.

'She was giving you the treatment, believe me,' I laughed.

Shortly afterwards, the baby in my arms and Yoshiye in tow, I took her to F's place for the first time. She really had put on a demure air. She opened and closed the sliding doors properly. Even the way she sipped her tea met every standard of etiquette. Nor did she talk much, and during the meal she was most decorous in the handling of her chopsticks. After a second helping of rice she said to the maid, who asked whether she wanted more, 'I've already had quite enough, thank you.' And so on ... I kept running a hand over my face in an effort to conceal my amusement.

So far so good. But she changed radically on her second visit.

The maid showed us in and we were standing in front of F's study door when Yoshiye said, 'Hi there!' in a tone that salesmen often use. 'Everybody's here. We're coming in, okay?'

'Please, do come in.' F answered in his normal gentle voice. Once we got in Yoshiye began. 'Oh, you've got ink on the tip of your nose.' Her eyes darted restlessly around the room. 'I'll spread out the cushions, all right? Phew! There ... gosh I'm pooped. Where's your wife — taking a nap?'

'Hey, stop rattling on Yoshiye!' She was at it again. I glared at her.

'F does have ink on the tip of his nose and since his wife is ailing it's possible that she may be resting. But it's rude to say such things the moment you're shown into the room. Your choice of words isn't too good either.'

Yoshiye pouted in a huff. It was no ordinary pout. She had deliberately filled her mouth with air and puffed her cheeks out.

F eyed the two of us with a smile. Naturally, he found Yoshiye amusing. But certainly I must have been equally funny as I rounded in on her faults and told her what I thought. For me, however, it was definitely no laughing matter. Whenever I'm with others and Yoshiye is also there, I'm on tenterhooks all the time. I have no idea what she might say. That's why from time to time I really have to speak my mind and tell her to watch her behaviour.

I can't remember when, but once we visited my old pal A. Two young friends happened to drop in and we were having a lively conversation when Yoshiye, keeping an eye on A's wife as she went about her duties as hostess, said in that scatterbrained voice of hers, 'Oh, look, your kimono seam is split along your backside.'

'For heaven's sake!' A's wife, a lady with a mellow disposition, took it graciously as she stifled a smile. I couldn't help feeling embarrassed for her, and my expression betrayed my mortification. When Yoshiye saw the look on my face she winced as though to say, 'Goofed again!'

'Shouldn't I have said that?'

'Of course you don't announce such things like that in front of all these people. Discreetly take the person to one side and tell her quietly.' I said it as nonchalantly as possible. Yoshiye nodded and said, 'All right,' relieved that I hadn't yelled at her.

Going back to the incident at F's place, another guest appeared a bit later and we decided to include him and F's wife in a game of mahjong. Holding the baby, Yoshiye sat down near F and me and looked on. After she tried to muffle a yawn, she got up and went over to the window.

The game had progressed fairly well. We'd all become engrossed. F was winning. He had set out the Pung suit he'd drawn, saw that he had a good hand going into the second game, discarded a red dragon, and began to sing breezily, 'I was sold away ... ' At that point Yoshiye, who had been dreaming by the window for some time finished loudly, ' ... and I'm o-off.' It was absolutely unexpected. As we looked at each other with incredulous expressions, I yelled, 'Loony!' F fell over backwards roaring. His wife laid her head on the tiles and tittered. At length I even broke out laughing too.

I must admit I can't say I never wondered whether or not Yoshiye was loony. But judging from what she told me about her school days, though she had once played too much basketball and had come down with pleurisy, she apparently never had anything like meningitis. She recovered quickly from the pleurisy and her marks in academic subjects were surprisingly good. So she seems to differ from the usual loony. Generally speaking, she's familiar with everything that the average girl from an old-fashioned family was expected to have dabbled in: tea ceremony, flower arrangement, *koto*, and the like. But it's not clear to me why I'm always catching her in the act of doing such odd things. I keep trying to make sense of it.

Could it be that deep in Yoshiye's mind, somewhere in her unconscious, she never really assimilated the conventions of society? Despite being twenty-two, she continues to do odd-ball things, acting more or less as she pleases; could this be an innate tendency perhaps? It may be stretching things a bit, but that's my personal view. Whenever I match up my interpretations with concrete examples I think, 'Aha, so that's it!' She's only an average girl raised in an average middle class family, yet I find myself puzzled over her upbringing and the sort of life she's led.

But even Yoshiye knows that social conventions exist. Her problem is that she has not absorbed them in the least. She is aware of the *shōji* door, but once she slides one open she completely forgets about it. Wherever she goes, she immediately makes herself at home. It's not just a matter of relaxing. For Yoshiye it's the natural thing to do.

Once I was stretched out on the *tatami* in front of my desk, my mind a blank, when I heard her romping around in the next room. She was shouting nonsense: 'Wow, wow, wow!' When I looked to see what was happening, I found her holding her kimono up and dancing ecstatically, her fleshy thighs exposed. The baby was looking up at her, a vacant look on her face.

'You're crazy!' I yelled. 'What on earth are you doing, kicking up all that dust?'

Startled, she momentarily stood still. Then she said, 'But it's spring.' I was so astonished I could only mumble to myself, 'For heaven's sake, what is she talking about?' For it was clear from what I knew of Yoshiye's normal behaviour that she could only be doing it to entertain the baby.

I can be forgiving if I convince myself her attitude stems from that innate, untamed nature of hers: an incapacity to assimilate social conventions. That's why I am reluctant to criticise her in front of others (there are instances when I pretend not to notice; it all depends on the time and place), but I try where possible to leave her alone when we are home. From the point of view of somebody like myself — constrained for more than thirty years by social conventions which I lack the skill to exploit for my personal gain, somebody, in fact, who creates for himself one problem after another — Yoshiye's daily behaviour is really quite amazing. Nor have I myself always accepted social conventions for the sake of it. What is more, the mere fact that I've never been able to tolerate the great pile of conventions that weigh our society down means that inwardly I feel a powerful resistance to customs. But I do try, insofar as it is not unreasonable, to keep in line with what is expected. You see, I'm self-conscious about overstating my resistance, and if I give this feeling free rein I wouldn't fit very well into society (though I must say I do not conform at all as far as the idea of gaining anything for myself is concerned).

Yet, the fact is that my life has apparently been somewhat unconventional, at least in terms of my relationships with relatives or friends. I suspect that I'll probably have to accept without complaint the way they describe me as 'an embarrassment' so long as society remains as it is. I am reluctant to say whether this is fair or unfair. I merely wonder: Does my life derive from feelings generated by my work, where I am unable to achieve my goals by taking the conventional view? Or is there something within me that forces me to live in this way, that drives me to work?

*   *   *

I keep saying I don't understand Yoshiye at all. But there is one question that I find particularly hard to answer: What's the best way for her to conduct her life so that she might never ever lose her uninhibited nature? It's been nearly four years since we started living together. During those years we have had a child. But we still have little hope of escaping from the grip of our rock-bottom poverty. Yoshiye's behaviour and way of life haven't changed at all either.

After lunch I was warming myself by the *hibachi*, my mind

preoccupied with practical thoughts such as: Whom should I visit? What tactic should I use for borrowing money? Suddenly, I realised that Yoshiye, still at the table, had been repeatedly calling me. I had been so engrossed in my thoughts that I naturally scowled at her, annoyed by her persistence.

'For heaven's sake, stop it. What do you want?'

'Look, darling ... '

'Come on, I've already asked what you want.'

'Chopsticks. These chopsticks. I can't make one work by itself! You really do need two.'

'You what ... ?'

'The baby flicked one away. I couldn't be bothered to pick it up so I tried eating with just one. I tried everything, but it was hopeless. One chopstick won't work. You really do need both of them to eat. It's amazing.'

'For crying out loud,' I said as I gave her my most menacing look. 'I'm trying to concentrate, so keep it for another time.'

'You can't scare me with a look like that,' she said, clearly evading my glare.

'Just shut up!'

Still looking at me, Yoshiye silently retrieved her chopstick and resumed eating. Then she lowered her eyes but stole a quick glance at me from time to time; I ignored her and went back to sorting out the faces of my various acquaintances.

I picture myself in front of somebody who appears quite reluctant to lend me anything. I am saying shamelessly: 'Now they've turned off the electricity and the gas has been off since last month. Well, I may have been negligent about paying, but still it's not my fault things have turned out this way. I've got to live, too, you know. Don't you think I should at least have the lights back on?'

(MARCH 1934)

3

Guile

I don't mind being poor. But it's annoying when they turn off the electricity or when you're out of food. Being without food is the most miserable of all.

'Nothing left,' my wife said. 'Better go and rustle up something.'

'Leave it to me.' I zip briskly out of the door. My zip, however, lasts only to the alley. Beyond the alley I walk along scuffling my clogs despondently. But hands in pockets and humming, no one would possibly take me for anything but a carefree stroller.

During the past few weeks, I had already touched friends and acquaintances for loans, borrowing to the limit of our intimacy. That's why, to tell the truth, I'd run out of places to go. But I have got to find some food. So, too bad, I head for someone I know.

'Hi there! You're looking fine as usual.'

'Yup, doing fine,' I say. By nature I'm incapable of blurting out that I'm not doing well. I've always found it much easier to look cheerful no matter how badly off I am. That ends our conversation. I decide not to try and make a touch on this occasion and talk my head off instead all the more jovially before leaving. 'Be seeing you.' I set out for my next stop — of course I have no money for a tram fare so I walk. It's a long, long way.

Once I was stopping here and there on a similar mission, dragging myself all the way from our lodgings in Suwamachi, Yodobashi Ward, to B's place in Nakano. In those days, B was one of my more recent acquaintances, so we weren't close enough for me to ask him to lend me some money. I literally staggered up to his door. Once shown in, I found he already had three visitors. All acquaintances of mine, they were also destitute fellows in love with literature, though not as badly off as I was.

'Hey, you're a sight for sore eyes. Come on, let's get started.' B stood up, full of energy. From the assembled cast, I guessed at once that it would be mahjong.

'You want to show off, do you?' I asked.

'Well, you see, S here can't play and we've been itching to get going. Unfortunately my wife's out,' he said, getting the tiles from

the cupboard, 'so you couldn't have come at a better time.' He tied
the cover haphazardly over the table.

'Do I have to?' I mumbled, forcing a smile. The image of
Yoshiye playing with the baby in a corner of that shabby six-mat
room in Suwamachi floated into my mind.

'You're being awfully stuffy, aren't you?'

'I am stuffy! But I'll play on one condition.' It slipped out with
surprising ease.

B smiled. 'Oh, you want to raise the *ante,* eh?'

'More crucial than that,' I said, grinning broadly. 'Actually, if
I'm not back soon it'll be tough for the folks at home. You know
how it is. I'm like a parent swallow trying to feed the family.'

B, appeared a bit nonplussed, and rattled off incoherently:
'Nothing to it. If you don't mind, leave it to me. Not a thing to
worry about. Come on, let's get started ... just a second, okay?'
Then he went stumping down the stairs. After a short while he called
up, 'Hey S, come here a minute.' S went downstairs without
answering. It sounded as though they were discussing something
down there. Soon B came pounding back up the stairs. The moment
he sat down he rolled the dice saying, 'Come on, let's decide who
starts the draw.' He cast a quick glance at me and said, 'I've asked
S to look after it.'

'Well, that's a load off my mind. Okay, now I'll show you how
it's done.'

'You're impossible!'

The other two, who had till then been looking vaguely perplexed,
set about lining up their tiles like seasoned veterans.

*　*　*

This is the *modus operandi* with which I've somehow managed
to humbug my way through life. My wife at first seemed quite
shocked at the way I operated. I was surprisingly casual. Yet I always
made it one way or the other, so — because my work was slowly
shaping up as well — Yoshiye gradually stopped being shocked.
Even if she thought the situation was hopeless, when she saw me
grinning she apparently changed her mind. Before long she was her
happy-go-lucky self again. By the time the baby came along, we
were birds of a feather. All of which really put me on the spot. There
is no way I can always remain so indifferent, and thus at times I
unwittingly look sullen. Yoshiye exaggerates my sulkiness in her
mind and is immediately affected. When her man who generally
beams at everything sulks, she assumes it must be serious and she

becomes upset. She acts as though a gale has torn our roof off: 'What happened? What's wrong? What is it?'

'My tooth has been aching something terrible since morning,' I say, glancing erratically out of the window; 'it must be the weather or something.'

'Your tooth aches when the weather is so nice?'

'Seems like it. My teeth are odd.'

'How strange ... shall I get an icebag?'

'It's not that bad.'

'But it worries me,' she says — clearly relieved. Talking things over with Yoshiye, however, never settles anything. If I look drained, she shadows me. And being shadowed only makes things worse.

I dispose of the problem by saying, 'Oh, I'm okay. It doesn't really bother me. It's nothing.' Usually that's enough to get her to believe me. A curious woman ....

'If you're really healthy,' I said, 'I'm sure you'll have an easy delivery even if we don't have a midwife to look at you. Don't worry.'

'Maybe so, but when the baby is born we're going to need money, aren't we?'

'Right. I know things'll pick up. It'll be a once-in-a-lifetime experience for the baby, so I'm sure things'll pick up.'

'Yes, I suppose they will.' She was completely soothed.

Hers was, in fact, an extremely easy delivery. Yoshiye had read 'Guide to Easy Childbirth,' a supplement to a woman's magazine, frequently enough to have learned it by heart. Also, she had learned enough from the landlord's wife to make a self-diagnosis, predicting delivery in ten days. When I came home on the evening of that very day, she lay groaning in our dimly-lit room. 'Well,' she said, 'better call a doctor ....' I scurried off to the neighbourhood clinic and asked a midwife to come and take a look. She said the baby was on the way.

'Do you want it here, or ...' the midwife asked, and without hesitating I said, 'By all means at the clinic.' So far so good. The midwife hurriedly left saying, 'I'll get the hot water ready.' 'Do you want it here?' she asked, glancing around our six-mat room with its single *hibachi*, its single desk, but with no sign whatsoever that any preparations had been made for the delivery. 'That was definitely a sharp pain.' Yoshiye said standing up. 'Ohhh!' I insisted she lean on my shoulder as we walked the block or so to the clinic. I offered to carry her but she refused because it would be embarrassing. When we got to the clinic I let the midwife take over and went out to buy some baby things. I asked for the cheapest. Rushing back to the clinic, I found the atmosphere somehow different. Yoshiye, flat on her back, smiled faintly and said, 'It's over.'

'Really? Well, how about that!' I blurted out nonsensically.

'How do you like that ... really?' The midwife and her young aide
laughed jovially from the adjoining room. I went in. A little reddish
thing lay submissively in the hot water, being soaked in its first bath.
It is ridiculously long, I thought. Then, hey! I noticed it was a girl.

'Thank you so much,' I said bowing.

'You're welcome. It was really an easy delivery. A fine baby!'

'Indeed ....'

'The layette ... you're just in time.'

'Right ....' I scratched my head.

'It's a girl,' Yoshiye called from her room. 'Do you mind?' It
seemed a funny question because the fact was, mind or not, we'd
just had a little girl.

'A girl's fine. Look here,' I said, 'since my intuition's so good
I went out and bought a pink layette.' To put Yoshiye's mind at
ease, I deliberately dangled the padded cotton nightie (it had a hemp-
leaf pattern) in front of her, a triumphant look on my face. She
thought I would be mad at her for having a girl.

She stayed in the clinic for about two weeks. 'Usually it's a
week,' the midwife said, 'but if you want to be safe, it's fine to stay
ten days.' But I kept putting it off for one reason or another.

'In any event, it's her first. And the old folks aren't around, so
I'd like to play it doubly safe,' I told her. 'And this is a good chance
to go out and rent a house, too ....' But actually I was flitting around
here and there trying to raise some money. By the second week, I
finally got the necessary amount together. Without a moment's
breather, I left around six that evening to look for a house to rent.
At seven I found some accommodation with two rooms, one room
with six and one with two mats, making a total of almost 145 square
feet. I promptly brought in some rags and a bucket and cleaned the
place up. At nine I was in front of the clinic with a cab, which I
loaded up with Yoshiye, the baby, and all our belongings. I sat in
front with the driver. We managed to check out of the clinic and
move at the same time.

'How do you like it? It's ground level, not a flat. Those boarding
houses — are rubbish!' I was so desperately tired I had lost control
of my tongue.

'Hmmm,' Yoshiye said, raising her head from the quilts where
she had stretched out the moment we arrived. She peered around
the place before asking, 'What's the rent?'

'Twelve yen. But I got them to come down to eleven. Later on
I think I can get them down to ten.'

'Some places are dirt cheap, aren't they?'

'Right. It's a real find at the price.

'Cheap, but ... terribly shabby, isn't it? Could it be because I'm seeing it at night?'

'Not at all,' I said. 'Houses always look much shabbier in the daylight. I'll have another go at cleaning it tomorrow. It's only temporary. We'll just have to make do.'

'Of course I don't mind. But ... ,' she was on the point of saying something when she broke out giggling. I thought she'd never stop.

'Oh, come on, stop it,' I said as I broke out laughing too. In any event, this was the first house I'd rented since we go married.

Most important of all, the baby was in the pink of health and the mother was also doing extremely well. I didn't let Yoshiye out of bed for a whole month, and the two weeks after that I had her take things easy so she was soon as fit as ever. She was so healthy that, on average, she had to throw away three-quarters of a pint of her milk every day.

'How about that, eh? Didn't everything turn out well? I worked it all out without a hitch.'

But for all my boasting, the rent soon went unpaid for several months and, when the merchants no longer made deliveries, I became increasingly concerned about how Yoshiye was taking it. She often had nothing to eat till supper. This put me in a quandary because, while it was obviously bad for her, it had an immediate effect on the baby. My first concern was Yoshiye's milk.

As the baby grew, we threw less and less of the milk away. But Yoshiye's supply remained plentiful. When she went to the public bath-house, white streams spurted from her nipples. The baby clamoured for it with delight. Yoshiye felt contented, too, squirting it into a handy wooden pail and sporting with the baby. She said some woman in the bath-house eyed her enviously, which is quite easy to understand.

But with no food, even that amount of milk would ... well, in a word, when Yoshiye went hungry her milk would suddenly dry up. Because the baby couldn't get a drop no matter how hard she worked, she became irritable. I had heard such things could happen but never imagined I might actually run into the problem myself. I was puzzled.

Whenever that happened, I went out and returned shortly after with some food (I couldn't very well come back without any, so, whatever it took, I'd get hold of some). At the sight of food, milk started trickling drop by drop from Yoshiye's nipples.

'You're easily bribed,' I said.

'Naturally,' she answered shyly.

As a result of that experience I hit upon a cunning plan as a stop-gap measure. It was a matter of finding the right stimulus.

'It's happened again, darling, look ...,' Yoshiye announces -

flourishing her breast with the petulant infant in her arms.

I look as though I expect it and say agreeably, starting to get up, 'You know, I was just thinking of going out. I'll bring back some food, of course, but how about if I pick up some *botamochi*, too — the really rich kind?'

'*Botamochi* ... !' She immediately breaks into smiles.

'Right, *botamochi*. The kind they sell at Surugaya's on the corner. Theirs is the best you can get.'

'Right, the best.'

'You seem quite calm about it .... Well, I'm off ... hey! Isn't that milk?' I say, looking at her breast. A white globule appears on the nipple.

'Amazing!' Yoshiye looks down. 'Gosh, they're full, I wonder when that happened? Here, Kazuye ...,' she says, giving the baby her breast.

After these emergency measures I leave, definitely making it a point to bring back what I promised. If she thought I was kidding, she wouldn't produce any milk.

Then she began saying in deadly earnest, 'Darling, my milk's dried up.' Nothing of the kind had happened. It turned out she wanted something sweet.

'Yes, ma'am,' I'd reply, not even bothering to look up from my work, 'that's so annoying, isn't it?'

Sometimes, Yoshiye's craving for sweets amazes me. Once, I was leaning on my desk late at night, my mind a blank, when I realised that she was slowly sitting up in bed. Our place is quite small, so she and the baby sleep directly behind me. I turned around to find her sitting on the quilts, one sturdy arm and her torso out of the covers, one cheek wrinkled by the pillow slip. She was frowning, perhaps from the glare of my light, and she barely managed to get one eye open.

'Well, Long John Silver, are you awake?'

She wrinkled up her face, apparently at a loss for an answer. Then she abruptly announced, 'I want some *oshiruko*.' I glanced at her without saying a word. My first reaction was bafflement. I thought, 'She's at it again.'

'I want some *oshiruko*,' she said, unable to resist her craving. 'I'm hungry for *oshiruko*.' It looked as though she'd put both arms like props on her neatly parallel knees, but she intertwined them imploringly, her voice tinged with a peculiar urgency.

I looked at her gently.

'I'll get some in the morning. I'll get it at Surugaya's. How about some *dorayaki* with it?'

'But I want it now!'

'Now is impossible. A while back the clock next door chimed two. Nobody's up anywhere at this hour. If you go back to bed like a good girl, it'll be morning before you know it.'

Yoshiye gazed glassily into a corner of the ceiling for a moment, then blurted out, 'Ohhhh!' and pulled the covers up over herself again. That really was a close shave! Thankfully, once Yoshiye stretches out, she's asleep in less than five minutes.

It's irritating to be told she wants something and wants it right that moment. If I make a clumsy move when that happens, she becomes peevish. Since I get involved in her peevishness and become peevish myself, ranting and raving and on occasion even hitting her, I have to watch myself.

Once I had the following experience. It was cool enough to be wearing a lined kimono. Yoshiye had been fretting and fuming because I'd been unable to get her a short coat, a *nenneko,* to wear over the baby strapped to her back. She'd been pestering me for one since mid-summer. Somehow she realised that she couldn't rely on my customary, 'Don't worry, I'll have one made for you soon.' She was at it again one night when I had to go out.

'Well,' I said getting up to go, 'I'll be right back.'

'I'm coming too.' She looked determined.

'It's night,' I frowned at her. 'The baby'll get chilled. You stay put. I'll be back as soon as possible.' I said it forcefully.

'She'll be all right if I wrap her up well. I hate staying home when you're gone. Tonight for some reason I just don't want to be here alone.'

'Okay. If you have to, come along. But since I've got to try and get hold of some cash, for goodness sake, don't make a nuisance of yourself.'

'All right. All right.'

We left soon after. When we reached the Totsuka Circuit Highway, the wind that had not seemed particularly strong freshened considerably, producing swirling gritty dust clouds. It had considerable force. I turned up my collar and looked back at Yoshiye, doing her best to keep up with me, the baby strapped to her back.

'It's cold for the baby,' I said, with a touch of menace in my voice. 'Is she all right?' Yoshiye didn't answer. I walked on mumbling to myself, 'They'd be better off at home.'

A short while later Yoshiye abruptly said, 'Get me a *nenneko.'*

That infuriated me, but I stayed calm.

'Okay, I'll get you one. If I can scrape up some money tonight, I'll put off what I planned to use it for and buy you one.'

'Buy it now.'

'How on earth can I buy it now? Can't you get that into your head?'

'All the mothers are wearing them by now — I'm the only one carrying a baby around without one. I want one — now!'

'Can you imagine anyone making such a stupid suggestion in the middle of the street? Just calm down and be reasonable,' I said, turning towards her. 'Isn't that why I told you to stay home in the first place?' She had become a nuisance. Yoshiye stood rooted to the road, her eyes strangely tense. Though I knew I should exercise more self control, I suddenly lost my temper.

'Dammit,' I said sharply, 'go back home!'

'No! I'm coming with you.'

'When I tell you to go home, you'd better go.'

'I don't want to, she whimpered.' At that moment my right hand struck her face.

'Oh!' she cried out, startled, as she brought both hands to her face. 'That hurt.' She leaned against a nearby electricity pole and began weeping loudly.

I felt an ear-jangling rage welling up within me. 'Hell,' I said, 'I'll go back with you. Come on, get going. How the hell can I get money together like this?' I gave her shoulder a sharp shove. 'Damn you!' She tottered momentarily, but when she regained her balance she stood motionless again.

'To hell with you.' I stomped angrily down the street.

Yoshiye followed. 'Where are you going?'

I quickened my pace without looking back. Later, I found myself on the army rifle range. Trampling haphazardly through the tall grass, I noticed an embankment behind the targets ahead of me. It jutted high into the night sky.

I thought as I hurried along that I'd climb to the top. Hearing Yoshiye huffing and puffing right behind me, I swung around and confronted her, my fists clenched.

'Dragging me way out here,' she said, gasping for breath, 'out in this empty field ... you plan on killing me here, don't you?'

My fist whacked her head. She reeled, then steadied herself. 'So you are going to kill me and toss my body among the weeds here.'

'Oh shut up!' I said, grabbing a shoulder and spinning her around. The baby began crying and I found the sleeve of Yoshiye's unseasonal muslin *kimono* which I had inadvertently ripped off, entangled in my hand. With all my might I slung the sleeve into the grass and deliberately tore off the other one. Her fleshy arms, now exposed from the shoulders, seemed conspicuously white. I glared, livid with rage. She gulped in terror.

'A demon,' she screamed. 'Your face — like a demon's!'

Getting up she gathered herself and dashed impetuously through a patch of grass, then ran wildly across the bumpy field crying something like, 'Creepy! Creepy!' As she retreated, I could see her head and the baby's head lurching violently. I heard the swish of sliding sand. Both heads suddenly disappeared. Then I saw her crawling up the other side of the hollow.

'Mummy!' Her shriek caught me quite by surprise.

'Mummy! Mummy!'

Suddenly, I realised what a terrible experience this must be for her. I rushed off after her.

Cries of 'Daddy! Daddy!' ... were scattered by the wind.

Overtaking her, I caught her hair and forced her down. She settled and stayed put on the ground. I sat down, crossing my legs and wondered what to do next. As though obeying a command, I gazed into the star-studded sky. I felt the wind drying off my perspiration.

'Now look, we've both been acting like idiots. Let's calm down, okay?'

Rasping heavily, Yoshiye began to weep loudly again. Suddenly she stood up. I had to restrain her from running off.

'It's quite understandable that you often get hysterical. Come on, let's go home and I'll sit down and listen to all your complaints. Carrying on like this is bad for you.'

She bellowed most of the way. After a while, however, she seemed to take control of herself. At least she stopped trying to run off. Clinging to her sash, I pulled her through the field towards Suwa Shrine. Once we crossed the street in front of the shrine and walked to the far end of the compound, we'd be home. To get back to the street, however, we had to descend an eighteen-foot embankment. I went down first. Yoshiye had come about half way when she lost her nerve and froze. If one isn't careful on such steep inclines, it's possible to slip and fall. She looked ludicrous flailing those fleshy arms, bare to the shoulders, as she attempted to keep her balance.

'Here, grab hold,' I said, stretching out my arm. She took it with both hands and skittered down, looking as though she'd fall headlong. 'Gotcha!' I said, checking her as she reached street level. She laughed feebly, her face still streaked with tears, her nose running. Under the bright street light by the shrine, she could see those plump arms clearly exposed in front of her. She looked down at her right arm, then at her left.

'Look at me!' She broke out crying again.

'Stop crying. What if somebody comes?'

'This *kimono* ... I bought it to match Murata Osada's when we were in the fourth year of girls' school. It's the only one I have left.'

'I'm sorry about that. But come on, let's hurry home. You're probably chilled with what you've got on.'

When I put her to bed I told her not to worry, promising to bring her some *dorayaki*. Then, once again, I set off to try and get hold of some money.

Even if one is young (Yoshiye was nineteen then), having become a mother ought to make a person a bit more mature, but when the baby refuses to stop crying, Yoshiye gets all choked up with emotion and begins to sniffle. I can't turn a deaf ear to that, so I drop whatever I'm doing to humour the child. But it simply amazes me to think that I have to humour the mother first.

In a word, she is usually a pain in the neck! There are occasions, however, when she seems bewitched and uses normal language — almost as though she were a normal woman. What a spectacular transformation that is! These transformations weigh on my mind these days. That's actually why I am inclined to try committing them to paper.

— 2 —

I remember how we used to march in our gym classes when I was in grade school. Some classmates started out with their right foot when they ought to have begun with their left. Or, there were others who,though hands and feet are supposed to move alternately, managed to move their right hands with their right feet. For the most part, Yoshiye's daily behaviour reminds me of the latter. I haven't made any particular effort to select and arrange the episodes I've been describing. Whichever day you choose, that's more or less how she behaves.

Well, these transformations of hers — I'm not imagining them, am I? — even affect her facial expressions. They happen like this: She grins in an oddly deliberate manner. I suddenly become aware that she's looking at me intently and smiling. Naturally, that puts me on my guard. I look back at her with a big grin. Sometimes I manage to distract her, but these incidents affect my moods. I feel that I've been truly check-mated, not by Yoshiye but by whatever controls our lives.

The following story illustrates what I mean.

Three or four of us were drinking at A's place, an apartment-style lodging house. On the way back from the toilet I stopped off at the drying balcony on the second floor to get a breath of fresh air. Suddenly I felt sleepy so I looked around for an empty room. I thought I'd rest a moment, but before I knew it I was sound asleep. A and the others began to worry about me when I failed to return. After a while, the three split up. One went as far as the railway line looking for me. They say that A even lit a candle and looked down the toilet for the dark blue, white-splashed kimono I was wearing. Someone suggested that I might have gone home. The trio, hoping to put their minds at ease, rushed by taxi from Ikebukuro to my house near Suwanomori. Yoshiye and the baby were fast asleep. It was almost midnight. When my wife heard their account she didn't chatter on as usual but gave some thought to the problem before asking, 'You did check the second floor, didn't you?'

'No, we didn't,' A answered, taking heart. The three hurriedly retraced their steps and found me. A's wife then described how, when they rushed to the top of the stairs, all worried but hopeful, they were surprised to hear loud snoring. She scowled at me through her smile.

'What a laugh! Three grown men chasing around for almost an hour — wish I could have seen your anxious faces. A picnic, a picnic! ... Let's have a few more drinks!'

'What a conceited bastard!' The three glanced at each other. They were completely sober by then.

'We've given Ogata another feather for his cap, A said, smiling through his irritation.

I arrived home singing lustily. Yoshiye had changed into an everyday kimono and dressed up the baby in her Sunday best. She was waiting for me.

'Hey, aaa...re you goin' ou...out?' I asked.

'No, I am not.'

'So, why the airs and graaa....ces? ... But boy, was that a picnic! Damn it, they were in a tizzy! How about that, didn't they look upset? Really something!'

'Please hurry and get to bed.'

'Hey, the quilts are laid out already, aren't they? Here ... isn't this your bedding?'

'It's yours. I'm going to put mine down in a minute.'

'Really? Well, if you don't mind. Say, Kazuchan, Kazuye! Hey, babababa!'

'She's asleep so please be still, won't you?'

'Did ... did ... didn't notice. Well, good night.'

'Good night.'

The next morning Yoshiye told me that, judging from the flustered manner of my friends, she imagined I'd end up coming home dead. Had I been brought back feet first, she assumed she had no choice but to resign herself to everything from A to Z — though she wasn't sure what that meant. After giving it more thought, it seemed almost likely that I would come home a corpse. If, so, since it was a waste to put a corpse on good bedding, she laid out

our most ragged quilts, so threadbare that one could burn them with
no regrets. She used brand-new sheets, though.

Still stretched out in bed puffing on a cigarette, I thought back
over the events of the previous night. A broad grin swept my face.
'Really? You're not kidding?' I said, springing up and turning the
quilts back. They were in tatters.

'You're too much!'

Yoshiye smiled, but didn't respond.

'You aren't leading me on now, are you?'

'No, I really had to be prepared.'

'Hmmm.'

'After you got into bed last night,' she said, 'you were mumbling
something about "Let well enough alone ... don't stir up the hornets
... oh, heaven forbid, heaven forbid!"'

'... I don't remember.'

'I thought of telling you that what you don't know doesn't hurt,
or that everything turned out fine, but I changed my mind.'

'You did? I'm glad you didn't say anything.'

'So am I. Instead, after I got into bed I said it softly to myself.
Then I calmed down and went back to sleep.'

We finished breakfast without saying much more. Yoshiye then
promptly got on with her housework.

She always pours herself into me like water. But once or twice
a year she freezes into a solid chunk of ice. Whenever I move, that
chunk — matching its container — clinks with a chill against the
inside of my head. Yoshiye is quite self-consciously normal at such
times, and her use of language is faultless. I can only imagine from
her modest smiles that she's making a fool of me.

What's the origin of Yoshiye's transformations? She becomes
completely independent of me when they occur. I may be going too
far, but maybe it's her own peculiar way of getting off by herself.
When she's sick of my company or when she cannot possibly be
with me, she can freeze up with remarkable ease. It's quite possible
to view this 'ease' as meaning she's ready to freeze at any time.

I have the discouraging habit of spending the daylight hours in
a complete fog, unable to get involved in work until late at night.
On one occasion I'd been working four or five days straight on an
urgent job. Having arrived at a break, I tossed down my pen and
flopped over backwards on the mats.

'How about that! The first section is done!'

'Darling ....'

It was Yoshiye's voice coming from the other side of the baby's
head. I had guessed she was asleep. From her tone I thought, 'Here
we go again.'

' ... have you finished your work?'

'Mm, part of it.'

'Okay to talk a bit?'   .

'Fine ... go ahead. Talk all you want. I'll listen.'

Yoshiye put the baby pillow under Kazuye's head, pulled out her arm, tucked the blankets around the baby, and came over to sit down in front of me. She wore that transformed smile of hers. I looked at her seriously.

'I've just been thinking,' she said leisurely, 'about Murata Osada, her big brother, and big sister.'

'Oh?'

'Their mother and father died when they were young, and they've been huddling together by themselves ever since. They're not particularly badly off financially, but they have no family to stand up for them. And Osada's brother is still at college and doesn't know anything about the world ... and besides, both parents died of T.B. so the kids have that cloud hanging over their heads. When I was living in Kanazawa, their house was nearby, and since Osada was a classmate I used to go over to play. I tried to amuse them. I'd just ... well, I'd just get everybody going. In the end I would even make Osada's big sister laugh. They told me that when I came over it was like having a house full of flowers. I really wanted to get them over their blues. Since that's the kind of relationship we had, both Osada and her sister cried when I told them I was leaving for Tokyo.'

I nodded, looking at Yoshiye's slightly tearful eyes.

'Honestly, I wonder what they're doing now. Osada's sister was supervising the salesgirls at a department store in Imaichi, but ... she said she'd never marry till her brother finished school ... and when I had that squabble with mother and decided to come to Tokyo, I had Osada's brother in mind. He doesn't know a thing about it, and I never told him either, but I believed that if things didn't work out for me in Tokyo he'd somehow help me out. In those days,' she smiled faintly, 'in those days if you hadn't appeared I'd long since have married him.'

Yoshiye had lost her father when she was six. Her mother, who had been his second wife, saw her through girls' school with what they had inherited from her father. But Yoshiye simply did not get on very well with her mother. One day, Yoshiye broke through her pent-up feelings and announced she was going to Tokyo: 'I can look after myself.' In cases like that, she was not one to give in — regardless of what others said.

A young friend of mine was managing a mahjong club near Waseda University at the time. His wife was one of Yoshiye's classmates. Yoshiye came to Tokyo at the age of eighteen, the July after she finished her schooling. She settled down in the club, which was closed because the students were on summer vacation. Using the money she brought with her, she jauntily went around sightseeing here and there. Towards the end of August my friend fell out with his parents over his wife, so he left home and took lodgings in the Yodobashi area. Of course Yoshiye tagged along and rented a room in the same place. When, at the request of my friend's parents, I went to prevail upon him to return home, temporarily at least, I found the young threesome blithely discussing how they planned to make ends meet. My friend didn't seem in the least inclined to go back home, and his wife actually talked of working as a hostess at some bar. Yoshiye laughed, prepared to try anything as long as she could do it with her friend.

Yoshiye becoming a hostess — well, as I saw it, she was absolutely not cut out for that type of work. If she becomes a hostess now, I thought, it won't work out. I knew it was none of my business, but when I first found myself thinking such thoughts I then realised my interest in her. So, when she was talking about 'those days,' those are the days she was referring to.

'The two of us, Osada's brother and I, never really talked very seriously. We were just extremely noisy. Still, I always thought he was the one I'd marry. I'm not sure, but I wonder whether he didn't feel the same about me .... You're not upset, are you darling?'

'No, not in the least.'

'Really ...? Well, on one occasion he turned up when we were living at the Shunkōkan. Remember? That's the time he took me to the movies.'

'Yes, I remember. It was raining. I believe you came back by taxi.'

'Right. That's when he told me that when he went home to Kanazawa for the summer holidays my mother came to see him to talk about me. She cried a lot. And you know, she told him she'd sent me an angry letter but she was resigned to my staying in Tokyo. She told him she hoped I'd be a good girl. Since mother's so terribly stubborn, there's no way she could wish me well to my face. She assumed that if she told him, he'd sooner or later pass it on to me. Before she left, I understand she told him she felt sorry for him.'

'Oh?'

'When I heard she had seen him it really irritated me. Can you imagine, saying such things to Osada's brother — straight to his face?'

'Well ....'

'She should keep her mouth shut about such things. If she had, Osada's brother and I could have continued being casual about our relationship. And that would have been the end of it. Just because a person is frank is no reason to go around meddling. He told me about it with a smile, as though he'd heard something unexpected ....'

'Sounds pretty complicated.'

'You know something else? Sometimes I can't bear you. I get sick and tired of you and often feel like rolling around on the ground. You know, it's usually after you've given me a good telling off .... And sometimes I feel as though this is all a dream, having a baby and everything, and I might wake up suddenly and find myself back in Kanazawa having some noisy fun with the Murata girls .... I suppose I'm bad and deserve to be told off for thinking like that.'

'Now listen here,' I said smiling as I recrossed my legs, 'I've told you before that you're not bad. You may have your faults, granted, but you can't help that. You ... well, it's not a matter of being good or bad. What shall I say? .... You're not tarnished, you're unadulterated.'

'Oh, lord, that sounds odd. I don't know what you mean.'

'Well ... in any event, getting back to the Murata boy, it's natural that you'd fall for him. However — while there's no reason for me to regard it lightly — it's the sort of thing, you know, that gradually fades away. Sooner or later you'll forget about it completely. Or perhaps it may survive as a beautiful memory. Actually, it isn't a question of what happens to your feelings. The issue is rather that you do at times hate me, that you get sick and tired of me, and at such times a number of things creep into your mind. Even feelings about Osada's brother, for example.'

I paused momentarily before continuing.

'The fact that I'm poor. The fact that there is quite a gap in our ages — these are certainly bitter pills for you. There's no need to harp on the bitterness of our poverty. But it's because of the age gap that our love for each other is not in better balance. Or rather, I should say that the nature of our affection for each other differs. For example, you just asked if I was upset, right? I'm not. That's the sort of thing I mean. When we have words, you might consider it a row when all I'm doing is reprimanding you. As far as love is concerned, I suppose that's my way of showing affection. But in plain language, I'm not very romantic about it, which probably disappoints you. That may be why memories of the Murata lad surface sometimes.'

'Could be.'

'I look young, and actually I'm quite vigorous for my age. For some reason, all my romantic sentiments have just about withered on the vine. I guess that's because dad died right after I turned twenty and I had to father all my younger brothers and sisters. Even though I told myself quite categorically that romance was impossible under those circumstances, I still could hardly avoid getting involved. And I failed with two or three different girls, one right after the other. Having been burnt, I was leading a peculiarly warped existence as far as my emotional life was concerned. That's why it's so hard for me even now to be on an equal footing with a young woman like you. Speaking quite frankly, it's a great pity.'

'It is. It certainly is. But ... why not leave it at that? I'm satisfied.'

'Having come this far, what could you say? Anything else would be expecting too much.'

'Things will pick up,' she giggled, using my stock phrase. That made me smile, but I soon changed to my serious 'nevertheless' expression.

'Tonight we've not really left well enough alone ... but since there's not much danger of getting stung, I might as well stir up another hornet. At first glance, we both seem happy-go-lucky. You would at least qualify as an optimist while I'm ... well, you might say that I'm at least working at it.'

'But aren't you twisting things a little?'

'On the contrary. You — the usual you, the one I keep calling a silly whatsit or a headache — quite frequently dance to my tune.'

'How true.'

'But you say "How true" only when we're talking as we are now. You're never aware of it when it happens. Recently, for instance, I was shouting commands at you such as, 'Tenshun! 'Bout turn! Remember? I was deep in thought at the time and, since you were chitter-chattering about nothing in particular, I chose that way to shut you up. That startled you and riveted your attention. I'm sure it made you think back to your girls' school days in gym class — eyes fixed dead ahead, a serious look on your face, trying to adjust your toes to the necessary forty-five degree angle. At such moments there isn't a shred of guile in you. No dissembling whatever.'

'Hmmmm.'

'You automatically dance to my tune. When you do, we're in harmony. But, you know, every once in a while when you start talking sensibly as you're doing now, you seem to withdraw. That's something else that can't be avoided, I suppose ....'

In the meantime Yoshiye had returned to her usual expression. She yawned and said, 'I think I'll go back to bed.'

'Sleepy?'

'I've been sleepy for quite a while.'

'No wonder you became so silent all of a sudden. Well, go on back to sleep. Even you will gradually learn about the ways of the world as you mature. There's no way of preventing that.'

Paying no attention to me she said, 'Goodnight' and quickly

burrowed under the covers.

A person like myself, concerned primarily with his own interests, ought to cherish a relationship with someone like Yoshiye. However, since this world is not a place where people can survive if they don't act in their own best interests I have no choice but to keep a tight reign on her. Actually, everything I've told Yoshiye to date is, in one way or another, for my own benefit.

'Ever since I was young,' Yoshiye once told me, 'everyone always said what a naughty girl I was, what an unpromising, confused child. Even my mother and big sister said so. That's why I assumed I was bad. You and the Muratas are the only ones who told me I wasn't.' Strangely agitated at this point, I said then with some vigour, 'Come on, we weren't the only ones ....'

In any event, I imagined that I'd like at least to get to the point where we had enough to eat. With that in mind, I thrust out my arms two or three times — hup ... two ... — and went back to work. Somewhere a clock was chiming three.

(NOVEMBER 1934)

4
Land of my Fathers

Father joined the staff of the Shinto Seminary at Ujiyamada in Ise right after graduating from college. I was born on Christmas Day of that year, 1899 — the first son. Three years later, Seiko, the first daughter was born. A year later, mother returned to father's ancestral home in Shimosoga, Sagami, to take care of his parents. Father and I stayed behind. Hiroo, Eiko, and Masao was born in Shimosoga.

★   ★   ★

My grandmother died when I was seven. She was seventy-eight. Her hair, an almost uncanny jet black, was slightly wavy and cut in what we call 'bangs' these days. She had a frightening face and was very tall, but so bent over in her old age that Seiko could ride her no hands. On one occasion after she had locked horns with grandfather she slipped a dagger (in a shark-skin sheath bearing the crest of her parental home) into the front of her kimono sash and said, 'I'm the daughter of a samurai.' This strong-willed old woman became all the more perverse when she realised she was in the wrong. Yet her greatest joy was being asked to help others; she really put herself out for them.

Shortly after she took sick she announced, 'I won't recover from this illness. Leave me alone.' Even family members who at first laughed it off as a joke eventually became upset. I remember mother tearfully pleading with this old lady who refused to see a doctor, who wanted no medicine.

Grandmother smiled, 'One dies when it's time to die.' She passed on about a month later, her last moments being extremely tranquil. Three or four of her younger sisters, themselves wrinkled with age, wept over her: 'My, oh my, doesn't she look peaceful?'

When she died, I was on the second floor of the outbuilding straddling the banister. Grandfather came up the stairs as I was stuffing my face with sweets while counting the white sails in Sagami Bay and looking at the pine trees — some looking like a hand-written letter 'f', others looking like a slanted letter 'k' — lining the old

Tōkai Highway that ran parallel to the shoreline. Not even glancing at me, he made a beeline for his eight-mat room saying, 'Gran ... granny's dead.' Though a martinet, grandpa was weeping. I sensed that I was witnessing something terribly comical, but I stifled my laughter, saying to myself, 'If you laugh you'll get told off, so watch it!' Then I tiptoed down the stairs and went into the living room where I romped through groups of neighbours engaged in animated conversation.

★   ★   ★

Seven years later grandfather died at the age of eighty-six.

After grandmother's death, grandfather seemed to deteriorate rapidly. He no longer spent much time chanting those *Noh* plays he loved. Whenever it was even slightly chilly, he'd huddle the whole day over an out-of-season *kotatsu* trying to keep warm. I'd think he was sleeping when all of a sudden he'd intone: 'The willows are green, the flowers crimson.' Then he'd yawn like a canyon. 'Auntie' Otsuya, who had been around for years and whom mother trusted so much you couldn't imagine she was a servant, knew best how to handle grandpa.

He calls, 'Taikooo' (mother's name) from his room. Mother's 'Yes' and auntie's 'Coming' are simultaneous.

Impatiently on the heels of the first call comes another, 'Taikooo!'

Auntie says, 'Madam, let me go,' so mother doesn't have to drop her work.

'Okaaaay,' auntie says, raising herself laboriously from the mats, brushing down her apron, and flapping her hands behind her as she takes off.

'Yessuh? Did you want something, grampa?'

'If I call, you'd better believe I do!'

'All right ....'

'Some flies are pestering me. Get rid of them. There must be two or three.'

'All right,' sixty-year old Auntie Otsuya says. For about five minutes she thrashes wildly about with a fly-swatter, unconcerned about whether or not she hits anything. Then, back to work.

Some three years before he died, grandfather became paralysed. The paralysis affected the entire left side of his body and his tongue as well. Even with a speech impediment, he often grumbled. When the women were washing the dishes after the meal, grandfather's shout invaded the kitchen: 'When we eatin'?' Mother often gave him an enema. Going to get his medicine every other day was the vital rôle I played.

Before long, grandpa began calling out, 'Auntie!' It had become too hard for him to say 'Taiko.'

'Okaaay.'

'Auntie!'

'Okaay, right away,' she says, grunting as she rises from the mats.

When she assumes it couldn't be anything important, she stands at the bottom of the stairs and calls up, 'Grampa, did you want something?'

'Get up here!'

'All right ....' She has to be careful climbing the stairs.

'What did you want, grampa?'

'Auntie, what's the date today?'

'Today's the thirtieth, grampa. Last day of the month.'

'What's the date tomorrow?'

'Today's the last of the month so tomorrow's the first.'

'That's peculiar ....'

Auntie Otsuya stands silently a moment before she asks, 'Is that all you wanted, grampa?'

'Yeah.'

'All right, then I'll be going. See you later.'

She no sooner withdraws to the living room and sits down with a sigh then she hears grandpa's voice, 'Auntie!'

*   *   *

Every time I think of death, the calm way my grandmother died and the wretched last days of my grandfather come to mind. Grandma never gave an inch, and that's how she was to the very last. Now I can see why the end for grandpa, actually just as obstinate as grandma, seemed even to his young grandson to lack any self-respect. It was because of his paralysis.

Grandfather's obstinacy reminds me of the following incident.

One summer evening he told mother, 'Get me some red peppers.' She wondered what he wanted them for, but it was not her place to question him. She laid a bundle of shrivelled red peppers before him. Grandfather gave her a sullen look and threw the bundle into the yard-square zelkovia wood brazier that took the place of an open hearth in our living room. Mother and Auntie Otsuya looked at each other with troubled expressions. But they neither moved nor said a word. Presently, however, they could no longer endure the fumes and, gasping for air, got up and escaped to the kitchen where they ran outside through the back door.

'Idiots!' grandfather muttered in disgust, never budging an inch from the brazier and maintaining his sullen mien.

'I was wondering what he wanted them for,' mother said. 'Auntie, he just wanted a mosquito smudge.'

'You're right. That works as good as anything. But it's far too powerful for me.'

'I wonder if it's all right to go back in.'

'It's still suffocating in there,' auntie said. 'And look, grampa's sitting there as if nothing's happened.' The two women did their best to stifle their giggles.

It was obvious that paralysis had completely deprived grandfather, once such a martinet, of his willpower and his pride. With the screws in his head loosened, his normal ability to face life failed him. More than death itself, I dreaded the thought of living ignominiously with a mind that had gone to seed.

* * *

In the spring of 1916 father became ill. He resigned his post at the seminary and returned to Shimosoga on a pension. He died in February, 1920, nearly four years later, on the day of a heavy snowfall — rare for the Shōnan region. He was forty-nine.

Mother had cared for my peevish grandparents and her five children, looking after things during the absence of our father who stayed at the Ise seminary except for the end-of-term holidays. And now, shortly after burying the grandparents, she had to confront fresh hardships. But I'll forgo writing about her ....

* * *

I was born in Uji, a city on the banks of the Isuzu River. When mother took my sister, Seiko, to live in Shimosoga, father and I moved to an inn in Okamotochō in Yamada. It's now the mansion of a Diet member, but in those days it was the Sangūkan, quite a respectable inn. We rented a two-room bungalow. It faced south, a ditch marking the boundary of a spacious lawn. Rushes thrived in the ditch. The molted carcasses of dragonfly nymphs clung tightly to the tall, vividly green rushes.

Father frequently made kites for me. I was no good at getting them to fly. The ones that I couldn't get up fell and broke to pieces. Or, when after some effort I got one up, it wasted no time nose-diving into the ditch. But father kept making them for me one after the other, and since he also had some artistic talent, he often decorated them as well.

Students from the seminary frequently visited us. Because I was there they were sure to bring a box of sweets that might appeal to me. Father inspected each and every item, however, dividing them into those 'okay to eat' and those I 'shouldn't eat.' He promptly gave the 'shouldn't eat' sweets to the people who worked at the inn.

When it was time for father to come back from work, I stood on the bank of the ditch at the edge of the grass, watching intently for a glimpse of him walking along what they called the 'Back Road,' a short cut connecting Uji and Yamada. At long last, when I recognised his derby hat in the distance as he rounded the corner by 'Frog Rock,' I raised my arms and hopped up and down. Though I didn't think he could hear me, I yelled, 'Daddy!' He then waved his walking stick back and forth over his head and, quickening his pace, soon broke into a run ....

Father liked playing *go*. I missed him when he went over to his favourite competitor's house in Iwabuchichō. At such times, I played in the innkeeper's rooms with the lady who ran the inn or with the maids. But no matter how hard they tried to amuse me, I never really enjoyed myself. Once, bored stiff listening to the innkeeper telling me those dismal 'once upon a time' tales, I sat picking my nose and thinking, 'When will Daddy come back?' Sewing as she talked, the innkeeper abruptly reached out to trap something against the material. Then she carefully picked it up in her fingers and put it to her lips. I was just wondering whether — my gosh! — it might not be the bogey that I had just flicked away when, all of a sudden, she made a bitter face and quickly wiped the back of her hand across her mouth.

'I thought it was a flea,' she laughed. 'You rascal, you, giving me one of your bogies!'

The minute father returned she told him all about it. Smiling, he patted me on the head and said, 'You shouldn't flick bogies around like that.'

He often took me to Futamigaura. Once when I was trying to climb into a small boat that had been beached near the shore I banged my privates. It hurt so intensely I couldn't say a word. I just crouched down where I was. Father looked back, asking with an anguished look, 'What's wrong?'

Holding my crutch I finally said, 'I banged myself here on the edge of the boat ....'

'Those are your vitals,' he said, 'so you'd better take care.' He squatted down, offered me his broad back, and told me to climb on.

*   *   *

I changed schools twice, going to Numazu for the second grade and to Shimosoga for the third. Mother's parental home was in Numazu. Once while I was there, I happened to wake up in the middle of the night and discovered my grandmother — mother's mother — sleeping next to me instead of father. I wept silently. Soon after finding some suitable playmates, I perked up a bit.

Mother's parental home lay on the eastern edge of the city, facing the Numazu Girls' School located on the other side of the approach to the Hiye Shrine. The approach road intersected with the old Tōkai Highway and ended on the banks of the nearby Kano River. To the left of the huge stone *torii* spanning the approach, exactly at the intersection, stood a huckleberry tree that had soared loftily into the sky for generations. It served as a mile-post. At the right season the tree produced a super abundance of dark purple berries that attracted flocks of starlings and bubuls. (In some volume called *Source Materials on Japanese History* I later discovered this mile-post on a colour plate. Beyond that huge huckleberry tree one could see the second storey of mother's parental home; the pure white of the closed *shōji* doors made quite an impression on me.)

Kurose Bridge spans the Kano River there. I recall that it was the third span up from the river mouth. It was made of wood. On the other side lay Kanuki, and to the left, Kanuki Mountain with its expanse of pines. If I remember correctly, it cost five *rin* to cross the bridge.

I often played in a little boat near Kurose Bridge. In the spring I enjoyed fishing for fresh water sweetfish. Six or seven flies ran out like branches from my line of silkworm gut. My pole, made of bamboo, was three to four feet long. I caught a number of beautiful sweetfish just by skimming my flies over the surface of the water. The fish tasted bitter so I didn't eat many of them, but my grandparents soaked them in vinegared *miso* paste and ate them with gusto.

At the end of each term father came home from Ise, stopping off at Numazu for a night or two. Then he took me with him to Shimosoga. When his holidays were over, I left Shimosoga with him and he dropped me off at Numazu.

★ ★ ★

When I came to live in Shimosoga I experienced the misery of children who change schools. I had been brought up in a city, small as it was, and just couldn't get along with kids who had, as it were, grown right out of the soil. On top of that, grandfather was such an old crab that he never indulged me as father did. I drearily awaited

RG—F

father's holidays.

Around the middle of July, when it was time for him to come home, I never failed to get lacquer poisoning. Shining with vaseline, my face puffed up as though I had the mumps, I cheerlessly looked forward to his return. When the *jinrikisha* man walked through the gate with the luggage, I dashed to my room and, as the clamour of voices greeting father filled my ears, lapsed into gloom.

'Kazuo! What's the matter, Kazuo?' It was mother's voice. Reluctantly I went to the front door. 'Where've you been? Hurry and welcome your father back.'.

Wearing shy expressions, my brothers and sisters sat close together on the mats in our huge entrance hall.

'Welcome home,' I said insipidly.

Father only nodded. But as he was peeling off his gloves he said, 'What's wrong with your face?'

'It's nothing,' mother responded, 'just his annual case of lacquer poisoning.'

'Oh, really? But Kazuo, isn't it funny that you're the only one who gets it? I wonder why.'

'I wonder, too,' said mother laughing. Father also laughed, saying, 'Well, first things first ...,' as he headed for grandfather's room on the second floor of the outbuilding.

The hills and fields of the Shōnan region teem with wild lacquer trees that sprout fresh buds in April or May. By June or July their rich foliage throbs with vigour, their bark glistening gray and brimming with poisonous sap. The men who collect the lacquer girdle the trunks with small hook-shaped knives. In no time white sap fills the grooves. The men gather the sap with spatulas.

I shuddered whenever I met those fellows carrying their lacquer pails. On exposure to air, the white sap turns black and bubbles as it thickens mud-like in the pails. During the harvest period I wonder whether the whole region wasn't faintly rife with poisonous lacquer fumes. I never could get accustomed to such a smell, so all my precautions were to no avail. I hated the doctor who flippantly told me, 'Oh, you'll develop a natural tolerance to it.'

It was when I was in third grade, I think, that I remarked out of the blue to my father: 'I wonder why there are rich people and poor people in the world. If only the rich would give some of their money to the poor.'

Father looked at me intently.

'Kazuo,' he said gently, 'did you think that up yourself or did somebody put those words in your mouth?'

'I thought it up myself,' I responded without hesitation, because I thought it an extremely good idea. Then, with a serious expression on his face, father began to set me straight on certain things. That is, he corrected the errors of my naïvely-mistaken theories (?) on equality; I was really happy that there wasn't the slightest trace of rebuke in his voice.

Father almost never scolded. We rarely heard him use harsh words. He absolutely never hit us. Nevertheless, we only responded to him with obedience.

Father was totally subordinate to his parents. He always wore a smile and spoke in a mild-mannered way. But on one occasion mother, herself in tears, told me, 'I found your father weeping yesterday. Grandpa has been so unreasonable ....' I looked with amazement at her for having told a grade-school child like myself something so astonishing. But, sensing that something was seething under father's calm exterior, I felt a lump in my throat. I felt that I should listen to anything he told me, but I wouldn't ever massage grandfather's shoulders for him.

Our childish devotion to father stemmed naturally from his attitude towards his parents. After I was in middle school, I gradually began looking critically at both grandfather's selfishness and father's gentleness. Father's smiling face sent us children the message: 'I'll never make a single unreasonable demand of you. Just trust me and obey. You've nothing to worry about.' When in later years I recalled those days, I could never remember father's ever having exposed his failings or weaknesses to us children. He was a typical gentleman of the feudal age. I am not capable of making fun of such ascetic convictions.

With a father like that, my heart sank to think that he might end up with grandfather's cursed ailment, with paralysis, and be reduced to similar misery. I fervently hoped father might die as I knew him.

As I had wished, father passed away before he changed. He never deteriorated. But he died much too young.

Father always went to Ise Shrine at the end of each year to pay his respects. He returned with influenza. Popularly called Spanish flu, it had caused a world-wide epidemic in 1919 and 1920.

His condition steadily deteriorated, his chronic digestive disorders aggravating the influenza. The doctor told us at the beginning of February 1920 that he was in a critical condition.

By then father had become skin and bones. He said to me as I sat at his bedside, 'Take this orange branch out of here. It's killing me.' I tried to imagine what he meant. When I asked, 'Do you mean the cushion under your hips?,' he nodded joyfully: 'Yes, that's it, that's it.' As I changed the position of the air-filled rubber cushion, I felt sad; his eyes were alert but his mind wasn't all there.

He hadn't been that way ten days earlier when he listened silently as I read to him from Natsume Sōseki's *I am a Cat*. After I finished, he said, 'In a word, it's all slapstick.' That gave me a start. I felt as though I'd missed my footing on the stairs. Father hadn't been bored. That simply was not the time to read him a book filled with witty humour. His mind had been bustling with thoughts about what would happen if the worst came to the worst. But then — then I knew from his eyes that he no longer had the ability to think about such things ....

On the morning of 8 February, father unexpectedly turned to me and gasped in short breaths: 'That ... you know ... that camphorwood box. I've put ... everything ... in order.'

'Yes, sir.' My whole being rattled with terror. I couldn't say a word. I stared at him, wondering whether I should dash out to get mother.

After a while he said, 'It's best to decide everything ... carefully ... on the basis of common sense.'

He closed his eyes. That evening he died.

*　　*　　*

Two or three days ago I received a photograph from my younger sister, Eiko, in Shimosoga. The five-by-seven print, taken from the gentle knoll in my hometown commonly called 'Daibatake,' looked west across the mountains of Hakoneashigara towards Mt Fuji in the distance. One could also see what appeared to be the dike along the Sakawa River, just this side of the mountains. The photo had been taken from the location on Daibatake that for generations has been our family cemetery.

The elements had eroded the Chinese characters on many of the tombstones. Our plot contained the monument, shaped like a Shinto shrine, that father had erected for his parents. And there, too, stands the stone I had set up for father.

I'd left my aging mother in my native village, a mere two hours from Tokyo Station, and had not returned home for all of six years. Having spent many idle years in the seedy parts of Tokyo, the photo made we wonder: Whatever do I hope to accomplish? What shall I do? Shall I go home, shall I go back and weed the graves?

A line of dimly-recollected poetry floated into my mind together with the bitter feelings of days gone by:

'Though misfortunes reduce me to misery ...'

Then I finished the thought aloud: 'My hometown is not where I should be.'

'I know that, I know that,' my wife said. 'I know that, it's from a Murō Saisei poem.' Then she started reciting it like a schoolgirl chanting from a textbook.

When she finished she said, 'How about that? Pretty good, eh? The "my hometown" he's talking about is Kanazawa, you know. Murō Saisei's from Kanazawa, same as me. We've got lots of great writers in Kanazawa: Tokuda Shūsei, Izumi Kyōka, etc.'

'Kanazawa's quite a place,' I said by way of response, my voice trailing off. 'And you're quite something, too.' Fearing the paralysis of a stroke, grandfather had never touched a drop of *sake*. He lived to the age of eighty-six, but what a sorry sight! I'll keep drinking. And when my time comes, maybe I'll have a stroke .... Let's see, how old would this one be if I were fifty now, I wondered, gazing at the newborn son asleep on my wife's lap.

(JUNE 1935)

5
Entrance Bath

One day, after I had just returned from taking care of some business, my wife said with a look that suggested she had been waiting impatiently for me, 'I need three yen.' I told her I didn't have it but, not one to be put off, she asked me to scrape it up immediately. She was extremely determined. 'Just a minute,' I said. I sat down by the *hibachi* and lit up a cigarette. As usual, I had been traipsing around half the day on one petty errand or another. Though I'd managed to get everything done, I felt ready to collapse. And apart from anything else, I was famished.

I quietened my wife down, who frequently dashes headlong into things, and asked her what she needed the money for. She wasn't about to tell me.

'Well ... there's something I want to buy.'

'I knew it. Like what?'

'Well ... it's something big, really big, although you can rarely get anything that big for just three yen.'

'There's nothing wrong with something big. What is it?'

'It's empty.'

'It's what?'

'There's nothing in it.' She added that it had a lid and that she could never carry it by herself. Finally she told me straight off that it was just a bath-tub.

The people two doors down were moving. Yoshiye had been told by the woman of the house that her husband, a policeman assigned to a nearby station, had been transferred; the family was moving closer to his work. The woman had said, 'We have this bath-tub, one we bought second-hand for five yen, but when we move we won't need it. Won't you take it off our hands for three yen?' 'Fine!' ... And so my wife had settled it with her.

'It's a briquette bath,' she added. 'Put one briquette into the burner — that's all you need to heat the water. It's really handy and economical. Takes no effort at all. At three yen it's dirt cheap. It's all right to buy it, isn't it? Even if you say no, I'll have to get the money together somehow because I've already told her I'd take it.'

'So that's it! All right, I'll get the money together. But right now get me something to eat.'

'Oh, I completely forgot about you. We've already eaten.'

After supper I played with the children. I was not much in the
mood to go out again. But I had no choice. I left around seven o'clock.

I went to the Taikandō, a second-hand bookshop, and raised
the necessary amount. An old acquaintance who loved playing *go*
happened to be browsing through some books. Since I didn't feel
like going straight home with the money, I spent several hours at
his place, just down the street from the bookshop. It was near
midnight when I got back.

Piled in front of our doorway, almost on the street itself, was
the bath-tub complete with accessories. I stood there momentarily
under the moonlight, gaping at all that equipment. On the way home
it had occurred to me that we hadn't thought of a place to put the
bath. The question posed itself again as I stood there; a bemused
smile appeared on my face.

My wife and the children were sound asleep. I put the exact
amount, three silver coins, by my wife's pillow and was about to go
upstairs when I changed my mind. I woke her up. She was rubbing
her eyes as I asked her, 'It's great having a bath-tub, but where on
earth do you plan to put it?'

'Put it? What? The bath-tub ...? Goodness, I never thought
....' She sat there contemplating the problem with the air of one
who had suddenly seen the light.

★   ★   ★

For the time being we decided to use the tub in our entrance-way.

Of course, the house we are renting has no facilities for a tub.
We should have considered where to put it before we bought it. But
my wife characteristically does not do things in a systematic way. In
fact, I'm a bit the same myself.

Though it can hardly be called a yard, we have some seventy
square feet of open space on the south side of the house. Our first
thought was to make a little shed for the tub and cover it with
corrugated tin. We had no trouble dismissing that idea, since, to say
the least, it would cost money. Next, we seriously debated setting
it up on the verandah facing the open space. But this, too, came to
nothing when we considered the inconvenience of filling the tub.
Besides, if the children splashed around we were afraid the whole
area might get drenched.

In the end, we decided to put the tub in our entrance-way.
Because the vestibule boasts some eighteen square feet of concrete,
there was neither the danger of fire nor the need to worry about

flooding. The only snag would be if visitors turned up. But we talked it over and decided to cross that bridge when we came to it.

Two or three days later, after I had just got up around noon, I came downstairs and saw that the tub had been nearly three-quarters filled. The water was already slightly warm.

'How is it going,' I asked, 'Is it going to work?'

'I put a briquette in about two hours ago,' my wife said triumphantly, 'so you will probably be able to use it around two or three.'

'What about the owner?' I asked, making a sour face.

'Well, today's the fourteenth, right? The owner left for the market this morning and won't be back until evening,' she exulted, 'which is why I got it ready for today.'

The person who owns the property lives next door; our kitchen doors stand almost side by side. All in all ... well, if our rent had been paid up there would be no problem but, in a word, my wife felt awkward in this particular neighbour's presence. Our landlord — or, rather, landlady — is a widow in her fifties. She runs a market somewhere around Nakano and rents out seven or eight houses in our neighbourhood, quite an able woman. With her bulk of 165 pounds she could, with one searching glance and that protruding lower lip of hers, completely immobilise my wife. It took great effort on her part to keep a step ahead of such a landlady and heat the bath in our entrance-way.

'Kazu! Kazuchan!' My wife called our five-year-old daughter.

'Whaat?' she answered, adding in her childishly-piercing voice, 'Is the bath ready yet?'

'Not so loud,' my wife said. 'Listen! Today we're bathing at *home*, but don't you go telling Mrs Kawakami! Don't say a word about it, okay? And you're to take your bath quietly. No messing about, is that clear?'

'Okay. No talking. No messing about.'

'I'm not joking, now.'

'I know.'

In the middle of all this somebody arrived, apparently to visit. Embarrassed, my wife retired to the kitchen. Tanizaki Seiji had stopped by on business for the *Waseda Letters*.

'Well, how about that, you have an entrance bath! How elegant.'

'Hardly elegant,' I said somewhat grumpily.

We went upstairs and talked for nearly an hour about the magazine. — Then we went to a neighbourhood café and had some tea. Later, when I got home, my wife urged me to take my bath.

I decided to bathe our two-year-old son, while my wife played with our daughter in the street immediately outside the door. It was their job to be on the lookout for visitors.

While I was splashing around with our boy, my wife propped our fulling board against the outside of the entrance-way.

'Can you see through?' I asked

'A little. This frosted glass isn't very good at all.' She then tried again to get the fulling board into position.

Soon it was her turn to bathe with our daughter while I played in the street, running races and the like with our son.

Inoue Kōjirō came bustling along, his tortoise-shell glasses sparkling in the sun.

'Hi!' he said. Since he seemed bent on going right into the house I intervened. 'Just a minute!' I said. I explained the situation and he smiled in amusement. He told me about the business matter he had come to discuss with me and left. A little later, three young chaps stopped by to see me, but I asked them to come back an hour or so later when it would be more convenient.

*　*　*

We probably used the bath in our entrance-way five or six times. We also continued patronising the public bath. In the meantime, the weather got warmer and warmer, and we decided to move the tub into our backyard. We didn't bother much about enclosing it but resolved instead to bathe at night.

The landlady had discovered long before that we had been bathing at *home*. Our daughter had let the cat out of the bag. My wife had been busy in the kitchen when she heard Kazuchan talking with the landlady at her back door, right next to ours. Our little girl spilled the beans. 'Know what? We got a bath-tub. But we don't make any noise so you won't find out about it. That's why you don't know.' Kazuchan is quite small but she's got a big mouth.

My wife broke out in a cold sweat. But by then there wasn't a thing she could do, so she took the bull by the horns and from that day on she no longer tried to conceal that she was filling the tub.

'I thought that if we didn't visit the public bath very often,' my wife said, 'it would look suspicious, so we went from time to time. But now that the landlady knows, why bother? I'll go ahead and heat up the water without worrying about it. I thought she would be furious, but Mrs Kawakami is more understanding than I thought.'

'Understanding my eye! I bet she was just dumbfounded and didn't know what to say.'

'I wonder ....'

And so, ever since we moved the tub out to the back, we've

stopped heating it up on the sly.

Directly at the edge of our backyard is some high ground covered with various shrubs. On the top is a path which runs parallel to our house, but it's a dead end so not many people use it. There is a kind of crude fence and a hedge of wild orange bushes as well, so our bath is not really exposed to public view. But if someone made a point of peeking it would be annoying. That's why, generally speaking, we bathe after dark. At times even the neighbourhood housewives come over to use our tub.

★   ★   ★

One night, some meeting or other dragged on and on and I got home around one in the morning. It looked as though the bath had been heated up for me. I was a little tipsy from the *sake* but decided to bathe just the same. One of my relatives had taken a hot bath right after drinking and that was the end of him. Since I'm conscious of my heredity, I'm usually finicky about such things. But taking a bath under the influence is even more delightful than a plain bath, so I indulge from time to time.

It was a beautiful starry night. It seemed to be raining with the music of insects. The gentle breezes of that early summer night refreshed my skin. I felt so lighthearted that I began to hum, slapping at a striped mosquito that insisted on attacking me. Before long I was doing my renditions of *naniwabushi* tales, traditional ditties, *Noh* songs, and the like.

I don't know how much later it was when, without warning, a sharp voice rang out from the path on the high ground above.

'Hey there!' It was our local policeman. 'You taking a bath?'

'Yes, sir.'

'Open-air bath, right? Better set up something around the tub.'

'I'll take care of it.'

'Anyhow, cut out the singing. It's nearly two o'clock already.'

'I am sorry. I'll stop.'

The policeman left. All of a sudden, it was no longer very much fun, so I promptly got out of the tub.

As I was surveying the scene from my second-storey window, my eyes happened to fall on the bath-tub directly below. The moonlight — when had the moon come up? — shone on the surface of the water. I'd gone off without putting the lid back on.

I grinned broadly, amused to think how startled the policeman was.

'We've been taking baths in our entrance-way,' I told the writer, Ibuse Masuji. He eyes bulged in amazement.

'Your entrance-way must be watertight,' he said.

My eyes popped in amazement. Apparently, he assumed that we had sealed up our entrance-way, filled it with water, and heated it somehow. No wonder he was astonished. Ever since then, whenever I have the chance, I trot out this story and annoy him with it.

(JUNE 1937)

6

Crickets

— 1 —

I can't hear the crickets chirping yet. Their season won't arrive for another two or three weeks. At the moment their small, wingless bodies wiggle and meander through the grass or the rubbish. Unless you look carefully, you can't tell they're crickets.

I have a habit of hunting through my eggplant patch early each evening for ladybugs or their larvae. Once some baby crickets darted out of the straw I had strewn around the eggplants. The tips of the crickets' long feelers were white; they moved briskly. Though I had no intention of capturing it, one jumped into my outstretched palm so I grabbed him. Calling off the hunt for pests among my eggplants, I went back into the house, told one of my children to bring me the insect cage, and I put the little fellow into it. The tin cage had been designed for a singing frog. It already contained an assortment of bugs: some cicadas, an iridescent beetle, a dragonfly, and a green lace-wing. The children had deposited whatever they'd managed to get their hands on. Because the fine lid was not in very good condition, they had wrapped a piece of cloth around it. On part of the cloth the lace-wing had laid some spore-like eggs; they actually resembled tiny flowers on long stems, what we popularly call 'udumbara flowers.'

'Is that a cricket?' my daughter asked. 'It's tiny.'

'But it's very strong,' my son answered.

'That's 'cos dad just put it into the cage.'

My older daughter was in her second year of junior high, my son a sixth-grader in public school. I assume the educational objectives of the schools these days encourage a child to 'observe' immediately any bug they catch. For myself as a parent, however, I concern myself with bugs these days only out of the practical necessity to rid the garden of those that attack my home-grown vegetables and give me a headache. That need naturally coincided with helping the children's observations.

'Hey you guys,' I said, 'don't go cramming all these bugs in here like this. Just stuffing them into the cage and looking at them now and then doesn't amount to anything. Look, aren't most of the cicadas and the beetle dead already?'

'We know.' The children appeared downcast.

'Only the lace-wing is thriving. Look at all the eggs it's laid. But you were just lucky with that one and can't take any credit for it. You caught a female — one that just happened to be ready to lay her eggs. That's not something you could have planned. You know, I hear that when these flies become adults they live only twelve to twenty-four hours. Have you heard how we figuratively describe the brevity of human life in terms of this lace-wing?'

'I have,' my daughter said.

'I haven't,' my son said.

'The cicadas and the beetle are lying there dead, and yet the short-lived lace-wing has properly laid its eggs, performing her duty. I find that interesting.'

They were silent.

After my speech I realised that I couldn't expect the children to fully understand the significance of what I was saying.

I changed my tone slightly and, to encourage them, said, 'Still, accident or not, it's great you've caught this lace-wing. Which of you caught it?'

'Keichan,' my elder daughter said, intentionally rolling her eyes and, in her childish way, giving me something that looked like a forced smile.

'Hmmm. So it was Keichan,' I said somewhat loudly.

'That's right. It was me. I caught it!' My younger daughter's voice came from the children's room in response to what I had just said.

'What the ...! Keichan, I didn't know you were there.'

'Yes, I'm colouring, see.'

'You are? My, you are quiet. You've been so quiet, in fact, I didn't even know you were there.'

'Here I am!' Looking as though she'd dropped what she was doing, Keiko who'd just turned six then dashed from the children's room and jumped up on me. Obviously she knew that her father was in a good mood, and she had quite correctly perceived that the situation at the moment stood in her favour.

'Well done, Keichan! Where did you catch it?'

'It fell from the light shade, see.'

'Really? That's marvellous ... look at all the eggs it's laid.'

'I've already seen them, you see.'

Her words brimmed with confidence, yet were clearly those of a child. Tacking 'you see' or 'see' at the end of so many sentences is a feature of the informal speech of the southern Sagami region

where I come from. In Tokyo, these words happen to be replaced
frequently by 'you hear' or 'hear.' Unlike our two older children,
who had spent their tender years in Tokyo and had already absorbed
the way children speak in the capital, our second daughter had come
to the provinces at the age of four. She had been exceptionally
receptive to these country expressions. These speech habits surface
particularly at times like this. I found it endearing to hear her childish
country dialect superimposed over Tokyo speech. It sounded like a
fresh language.

'This bug you caught, Kei, is pretty, isn't it? Its wings are like
thin silk and it's green all over. It's really sweet.'

'Sure is. I'm not scared of bugs like that.'

'This one daddy just caught,' I said, 'is really something. Look,
the tips of its feelers are white. It's tiny but lively. It's a baby cricket.'

'Huh, that's a cricket?' Keiko asked, unexpectedly looking up
at me. Suddenly, she seemed engrossed in thought, no longer very
interested in the cage. Noticing her expression, I couldn't help
recalling an experience that wet my mind like water — probably the
same one that had captivated Keiko.

Sure enough, she came out with: 'Daddy, in our old Ueno house
the crickets chirped at night, didn't they?'

'Yes, they chirped all right. You've got a good memory, haven't
you?'

I hoped my response would not inhibit her but rather encourage
her to reminiscence further.

'And I went potty on the cricket, didn't I?'

'Yes, you certainly did.'

'And in the morning daddy got sick.'

'Right, right. You remember everything, don't you Keichan?'

'A cricket was chirping. In the beans on the top of the air-raid
shelter, right? And I got out from the mosquito net and went potty,
didn't I?'

There is something precious in the expression of a child tracing
back the threads of memory, eyes fixed in space.

— 2 —

Somehow, I'd managed to keep going until the end of August some
two years back. But I could hold out no longer. I'd returned one
morning from standing in line to get my cigarette ration. As I took
a deep breath to inhale, my head began to swim as though I was
going to faint.

I'm not the sort who keeps a diary, but oddly enough throughout
1944 I kept one fairly regularly from New Year's Day onwards.

When I flip through the pages, I find the first mention of my condition appearing around 18 January: 'At the invitation of the Sumo Society, observe eighth day of the New Year Tournament. Meet H. O. Chest pains increase, no energy to talk with O. Remain half an hour; barely make it home. Leaving the house is forbidden.' Subsequently, there was no week when I failed to mention something about my sufferings. Though I had written, 'Leaving the house is forbidden,' my diary records that I moved around quite a bit. Aside from the turbulent conditions and the flurry of events that everyone experienced, for me, personally, 1944 turned out to be quite an eventful year. My younger sister, past marrying age, got married. That was in January and obviously a cause for celebration. But the festivities drained me considerably. The fact is, I've been a sick man ever since.

I went to visit Shiga Naoya on 28 January. Aware that I was ill, I called on him to say goodbye, for I intended to return to my hometown in the country where I might recover. I returned the following day, the 29th, and recorded in my diary: 'To Shimosoga. Intend to recuperate a while. Too many odd tasks, too many visitors, no leisure in Tokyo for taking it easy.'

But in the end I was unable to take it easy in Shimosoga either. I found myself busily commuting to Tokyo. Trivial tasks cropped up one after the other. In due course, near the end of July, the death of my close friend Y. A. proved the last straw for my already overburdened condition.

11 July: 'With Matsuye visit Y. A. in a.m. at Nihon University Hospital. Understand he's been in critical shape with gastric ulcers. They say the worst is over. Looks debilitated; optimism impossible. Ardently pray for his recovery. Matsuye promises to send his wife some onions. Take sword to be sharpened. Return to Shimosoga on the 3:55 p.m. train. Part with Matsuye at Tokyo Station.'

They say Y. A. was recuperating nicely from the operation. Apparently, he himself believed he was on the road to recovery. When he saw my pale face, he worried more about me than about himself. As a matter of fact, I had the feeling whenever I left the house that I might collapse at any time, so I made it a point to take my wife along as a precaution on occasions when I imagined it would be a fairly long trip. Such was the case on that day too. The Japanese sword was a going-away present for my wife's younger brother (twenty-one at the time), who we thought would be leaving soon for the front as a fighter pilot in the Army Air Force. On the previous day, 10 July 1944, I had attended a meeting where I heard from a lieutenant colonel on the Imperial Headquarters Staff that the entire garrison on Saipan had died honourably. The report appeared in the newspapers nine days later.

19 July: 'Public announcement of Saipan garrison's refusal to surrender. Can't suppress indignation. Couldn't something have been done? Drinking and carrying on next door since noon; why reprove such people? As Confucius said, you can't paint a crumbling wall.'

20 July: 'Announce resignation of Tōjō Cabinet. Decided in accord with policy of evacuating school-children to remove entire family to Shimosoga. With failing health, fruitless to hold out in Tokyo.'

30 July: '6:30 p.m. During supper telegram arrives: "Y. A. dead." Put aside chopsticks, stunned. Get ready to go out but give up the idea. Feel miserable.'

31 July: 'Early a.m. Matsuye to Shimosoga. K. T. stops by, asks me to write an *in memoriam* piece on Y. A. for the *Literary Patriots*. Afternoon, head for Y. A.'s place. Home at 9; find Matsuye had returned to Tokyo at 3.'

1 August: 'Can't move. In bed all day.'

2 August: 'To Y. A.'s wake. Back around midnight.'

3 August: 'Morning, S. T.'s wife has labour pains. In his absence, take her at once to Kikawa Hospital. Safe delivery of boy around 9. Matsuye looking after her. Afternoon, Matsuye goes as my representative to Y. A.'s funeral service; wanted to attend but cannot move.'

Primarily, I have chosen entries related to Y. A.'s death, but interspersed with such activities was a host of petty tasks connected with our evacuation. The item 'safe delivery of boy' concerns a young couple for whom we were go-betweens; the husband had entered the military service about a month before that, and his wife was living alone across the street from us. We had to attend to everything.

By then I had already sent the two older children to Shimosoga. I couldn't possibly leave their care entirely to my aged mother, so my wife had been commuting from Tokyo about every other day. I also forced my weary frame here and there.

21 August: 'Just before noon, Takeharu (my wife's brother) stops by. Give him the sword. He's delighted. Regrets having missed Matsuye (in Shimosoga). Evening, K. K. stops by. Feel miserable.'

22 August: 'K. K. stops by. Dispose of some books.'

23 August: 'Morning, Matsuye and Keiko return from Shimosoga. T. T. comes by before noon. Matsuye accompanies him to the Shitaya Ward Office; give notice that entire family will evacuate from Tokyo. Impossible for T. to rent a house.'

24 August: 'Finish documents for removal of Kazuye and Ayuo (two older children); p.m., Matsuye and Keiko to Shimosoga.'

25 August: 'Take ration book to rice ration centre. Terribly exhausted.'

26 August: 'Matsuye, Keiko back to Tokyo. Understand all notices re removal completed without a hitch on Shimosoga side.'

27 August: 'More packing for evacuation. Had already moved quite a bit, but lots of junk remains. For last ten days or so feeling rotten; pleurisy seems to have taken a turn for the worse — not just neuralgia. The war goes badly. No peace of mind.'

My diary contains no entry for the following day, the 28th. On the 29th I had written: 'Excruciating chest pains last night. In bed all day. The day to send Matsuye to Shimosoga, but I'm apprehensive; let her go, telling her to return early tomorrow morning. Decide to see to Keiko myself; she cuddles up in bed with me.'

From the following day, the entries were in my wife's hand.

— 3 —

Keiko's memories of the cricket at our old house in Ueno were therefore remembrances of the night of 29 August, two years ago.

When Keiko said, 'Mummy, potty!' I took her in my arms, got out from the mosquito netting, and pushed back the rain shutters. There was no moon, but the stars were shining. Almost a dozen kidney bean plants — slightly shrivelled — reflected the light from our room where they stood on dirt piled over the top of our air-raid shelter at the edge of the verandah. Their leaves stood perfectly still. From their roots came the 'lili-lili' serenading of a cricket.

'Oh, it's daddy. Where's mummy?'

Still half asleep, she sounded as though she had just become aware of me. Had I held her differently or could she tell from my body odour?

'Yes, it's daddy. Mummy's in Shimosoga. Remember? She told you this morning: "Keichan, be a good girl. If you don't cry while I'm gone, I'll bring back lots of corn and be home early tomorrow." Remember?'

'I remember.'

'Wonderful! All right, now go potty and then be a good little girl and go nighty-night again. Hey, a cricket's chirping. Let's go potty on the cricket. Won't that be fun?'

'That's a cricket?'

'Yes, a cricket.'

As we were talking I took off her pants, got her in the proper position, and had her go.

'There, you went potty on the cricket. Wasn't that fun?'

'Yep. But it's still chirping. Listen.'

'Yes, it's chirping. But that's because crickets are cry-babies.

Keichan isn't a cry-baby, is she?'

'Not me.'

Once reassured, she seemed willing to accept anything. I felt relieved. And it made this four-year-old creature all the more lovable. Pillowing her head on my arm and pulling the covers over her, I settled down into my own subdued sadness over being able to do so little for her.

My feelings then were surprisingly pure and simple. Had that happened to me during younger days, when I was still puffed up with ambition and believed all things possible, I certainly would have turned up my nose at such feelings. However, at this moment I'm a sickly middle-aged man who has poignantly experienced the truth that he is nothing special. I may cling to a modicum of pride, tempered by knowledge of my limitations, but even if I have a sense of superiority about my abilities, I no longer have the slightest concern for the poses or reputation that swell from pride.

As I was thinking these thoughts, Keiko had tucked a hand into my breast. She was already asleep. Looking at that serene face moved me as though for the first time to ponder the mystery of life. I stood before that mystery, as I suspect any parent in my situation would, with a sense of humility and acceptance. I found myself repeating over and over that I had had only good intentions, that it was only because of my ineptness ... and then I noticed that I had a considerable fever. I merely felt listless and had none of the pain that so often stabbed through my right chest, my right shoulder, and my right arm.

The next morning I collapsed. As I was moaning, Keiko awoke. She came over to me and asked solemnly, 'Does daddy have an owie?' Making a strained effort I said, 'Mummy'll be back soon' — to respond to the child and, at the same time, obviously to encourage myself. I looked from time to time at the clock as I eagerly awaited my wife's return. Soon the morning mail came. Among the pieces Keiko brought in with her 'Here's the mail!' was the issue of the *Literary Patriots* that carried my memorial on Y. A. My wife came about eight, as expected.

After ten days of absolute rest I gradually began to feel a bit better. On 22 September I could walk to our neighbourhood barbershop, and by the end of October we were able to evacuate from Tokyo. For the first time in some twenty-odd years I took up residence in my ancestral home in Shimosoga.

— 4 —

Around the end of last summer Keiko heard a cricket chirping and said, 'That's a clicker.'

'You mean that chirping?' my son asked.

'Yep.'

'No,' he corrected her, 'that's a cricket.'

Keiko meekly accepted being corrected by her big brother. 'Yep, right, a cricket, I got it wrong.' And then she said, 'In our old Ueno house a cricket was chirping too, you see.' Apart from being impressed by the accuracy of Keiko's memory, I couldn't help contemplating why that event had so etched itself on her tender mind. My own emotions at the time were, as I've said, pure and simple — precisely why they so deeply affected me. That, however, was my own affair, not something Keiko could know .... But the fact is that the entire experience seems to survive in the child's mind and even now appears to be sketched vividly in the space into which she had been gazing. Why? Had she perceived in her childish heart the extraordinary aura surrounding those moments? I couldn't be sure.

And now, more than a year later, the child once again brought up the incident. Frankly, I was pleased she had. There may be some special relationship between us, something that transcends flesh and blood — odd thoughts like this unexpectedly flit through my mind.

Soon the children tired of the insect cage. After they finished supper, the younger two started getting drowsy. Kazuye, our eldest, did her homework; my wife spread out her sewing.

'It's amazing the way Keiko so vividly recalls that cricket two years back. I wonder why?'

'Well ...,' my wife responded indifferently. I hadn't really expected an answer from her. I'd only intended to mention the experience the night before I collapsed.

'I was more or less prepared for the worst those days, you know. I thought, what if ...?'

'I had my doubts about you, too,' she said. 'After all, just being away one night I found your eyes sunken, your face drawn and deathly pale.'

'But you were smiling from the moment you saw me. I thought you'd be shocked to find me in the shape I was in then — and there you were, grinning!'

'That's a strange quirk of mine. When I was a girl I often went to funerals on mother's behalf. As I was offering condolences I'd find myself smiling. It embarrassed me.'

'Oh? They say that people who smile are frightened.'

'That's not it with me at all. Whenever I heard somebody had died, I'd find myself smiling as I said, "Oh, you don't say?" Humiliating! Gradually I got rid of the habit, but once in a while it reappears. Like the time when I found you that way.'

'Good riddance, right?' I said, though actually it was not something I couldn't understand. But I changed the subject.

'There are all kinds of crickets,' I said, 'but I guess the kind that chirps *lili-lili* is the one. That's the one Keiko heard.'

'There's that expression, you know, *"Tsuzuri-sase* — patch up something or other ...."'

'Mother's explanation was that they're chirping *"kata-sase suso-sase* — patch your coats, patch your skirts, winter's on the way."'

'Some chirrup loudly, like *koro-koro.*'

'They're Chinese crickets — whoppers,' I said. 'They don't give you the slightest sense of autumn.'

Before I could get the words out, it occurred to me that I seemed these days inordinately concerned with bugs or weeds or such things. You could perhaps say that although I claimed I wanted to exterminate the pests in my garden, my concerns were by no means limited to the insects on my vegetables. Tiny bugs and nameless weeds — puny, weak things I had never been aware of before — grew vigorously. Small or not, the bugs were dashing about energetically, alive. Watching life gives me a certain peace of mind.

In short, my concerns stem from finding myself debilitated and ready to surrender. The clearest proof lies in my physical deterioration. Plainly visible, there's no way I can conceal it. Next, the fact that we lost the war; that and the ensuing social confusion wilt my vitality. We're constantly told about regeneration and rebuilding, and when I think about it I believe in that as much as anyone, but in point of fact I can't lift a single finger to help.

My private dialogue on this problem goes in marvellous circles:

> 'No good thinking that way — I know ... Perk up and be positive — But I can't just now ... Well, what do you intend doing? — I'm at an impasse ... Your trouble is thinking you're at an impasse — But I am.'

In a magazine last autumn I discovered the following utterance by Kawabata Yasunari: 'I cannot help feeling these days that my life does not stand on the verge of some "new departure" — it has already ended. I can only go back now alone to the ancient hills and streams. Writing as one already dead, I don't think I'll pen a single line about anything but the beauties of this pitiful land.'

I regard this one of the most beautiful of all expressions uttered by Japanese authors after the war. But at this moment I can only watch helplessly from afar the vitality of regeneration and rebuilding. I can, moreover, only feel envious of Kawabata's words. They reverberate with an extremely sensitive insensitivity, articulately expressed; actually they are rather stately. But with my own mediocre sensibilities, I am incapable of uttering such striking comments, strung as I am between extreme sensitivity and insensitivity. My companions are small, helpless living things ....

I happen to notice my children, already sleeping soundly, their faces tranquil. Whatever will become of these creatures, now so small, so weak? I wish I could witness the outcome. It isn't that I worry about what will happen to them after I'm gone. I'm concerned rather to watch with my own eyes what each of them will make of life. And, since they'll be growing up in a changing Japan, whatever happens I must be sensitive to their experiences. The thought occurred to me that Kawabata certainly doesn't seem to have any children.

With that I recalled having overheard the doctor confidentially tell my wife, 'His condition isn't critical. He'll be all right for another five or six years.'

Picking up the insect cage the children had abandoned, I found the lace-wing had died. It lay there peacefully among the carcasses of the cicadas and the beetle. The eggs the lace-wing had left behind still looked like flowers. The baby cricket with the white-tipped feelers hopped recklessly around the cage with ridiculous energy.

'I wonder whether it's a Chinese cricket or one that chirrups, "*kata-sase* — patch your coats"?'

'I wonder ....'

There was no way my wife could have understood my question. I decided it was the offspring of a *kata-sase* cricket. In another two or three weeks I suppose they'll be chirping, 'Winter's on the way.'

(SEPTEMBER 1946)

7
This and That
About Bugs

One sunny afternoon on a day late in autumn, not long after a piece of classical music began on the radio, a spider emerged from a corner of my room and started making strange movements on the wall.

I'm just beginning my fourth year in bed. For every improvement I suffer a setback, although at this particular moment improvement seems to be winning the day. Yet if I compare the years, one spring with another, one autumn with another, somehow the prognosis of my illness isn't good. Perhaps I'm gradually deteriorating without being aware of it. In any event, these days I spend most of my time in this run-of-the-mill eight-mat room with many hours to stare hard at the ceiling with its two or three rain spots.

Since the days have turned chilly, one doesn't see any winged bugs around — except the flies that cling to my red-cedar ceiling. When the sun shines, they come down to the mats or wooden corridor along the windows and buzz about. They're a nuisance because they gather on my face.

Aside from the flies, I sometimes notice spiders on the ceiling or walls. They're huge ash-coloured ones flecked with light spots; if they spread out their legs to either side, these spiders can span the narrow part of the rectangular divisions on a *shōji* door. In all probability, two or three of them apparently hide themselves somewhere in my 9 x 15-foot room. They have never appeared together, but my discerning eye immediately knows which is which. I concluded that the one making the strange movements on the wall was the smallest of the trio.

The piece on the radio was *Zigeunerweisen*, — no doubt the twelve-inch Victor Red Label, Heifetz performing, which I myself owned some years back. Recognising it from the first bars, I cleared my mind and instinctively strained my ears to hear those lush melodies.

Staring at the ceiling, I soon became aware of something slipping smoothly into my field of vision. It was that spider. No sooner had he emerged about a foot from the corner of the wall than he abruptly stopped in his tracks. As I watched absent-mindedly, he began inching across the wall — as though warming up — slowly moving one long leg at a time. He's dancing! At least that's what I thought at first, though his movements were not so obviously synchronised that you could call them a dance. It was not so much that he responded specifically to the music than that, somehow or other, he walked aimlessly around a single spot with a jerky gait that looked as though he was fretting and fuming.

Part astonished and part amused, I imagined that he was certainly enjoying himself. This amazed me for another reason. I'd heard that music produced by human beings could excite cattle or dogs; in the case of dogs in particular I myself have actually seen it happen. But when it comes to this spider, well, I just couldn't accept my initial interpretation at face value. So I glued my eyes on him sceptically, observing him closely so as not to miss his reaction at the end of the piece.

When the music stopped the spider reacted abruptly. He stood dead still. Then, nimbly and rapidly, he slipped silently back into his hiding place in the corner, out of sight. It looked somehow to me as though his hasty retreat reflected an attitude of self-consciousness at being observed or discovered — well, to say outright that this motivated his response is odd, but that was certainly the impression I got when I watched him.

I don't know whether or not spiders have a sense of hearing. I've read Fabre's *Life of the Spider* but I don't remember whether he answers this question. Nor do I know if spiders have been provided with other ways of sensing sound that differ from our own. In short, I'm completely ignorant of the subject. But without grounds on which to dismiss what I'd seen as mere coincidence, my observation did produce a somewhat peculiar feeling. My first reaction was, 'Now you'd better start paying closer attention to those spiders!'

Talking of spiders, I recall how I'd accidentally shut one up for a time.

In summer when it's hot I usually have a bit more energy. Once I needed an empty bottle for some reason so I chose one I thought appropriate. When I casually removed the cap, a spider dashed out and disappeared behind something. From end to end of its outstretched legs it measured only an inch or an inch-and-a-half; flesh-coloured and slender, he was a midget compared to the fellows on the walls of my eight-mat room.

I was somewhat surprised that a spider had been in the bottle. I searched my memory for a clue. Early last spring, I had told my children to wash up some empty bottles and leave them upside down for a day or so in order to dry out. After that I capped them to keep out the dust and dirt and placed them all in an empty box we had around. The spider had doubtless got into the bottle as it dried out.

Having found himself trapped, perhaps he at first thought nothing of it. Soon, as the days dragged on, I suppose he got hungry and then realised his predicament when he tried going off to hunt for some food. When every possible effort to get out proved futile, he realised the impossibility of escape. Soon he stopped struggling. He merely waited intently for the opportunity to get out. And then, half a year later, he actually escaped from the bottle — a split second after I'd removed the cork. Only a sprinter awaiting the starter's gun can take off that quickly.

There was another similar incident.

A floored corridor runs along the south end of my eight-mat room. Off its western edge is a toilet. The window over the urinal faces west; through it one can see Mount Fuji looming over our plum trees. One morning I discovered a spider had been caught between the sliding window panes. During the night I imagine that I or somebody had opened the window. The spider had been on one of the panes and had become trapped when the window was opened all the way. This fellow resembled those in my eight-mat room, measuring some three inches from end to end of its outstretched legs. Although there was sufficient space between the two panes of glass to allow movement, the lined-up window frames did not leave enough room to permit escape.

I immediately recalled my previous experience with the spider in the empty bottle. I hit on the idea of observing what might happen to him. I ordered everyone in the family to leave the window alone. The spider in the bottle hadn't eaten a thing in about six months, having kept himself alive on the air that leaked through the small spaces between the neck of the bottle and the rough wooden stopper. This fellow in the window was quite plump and far bigger. I thought he'd be able to outlast the smaller one if I put him to the test.

The Mount Fuji I see every time I go for a pee takes on various aspects depending on weather and time of day. On clear days, the mountain doesn't look like anything special. But in the dead of night, Fuji glimmers dim and silent under a cloudless moonlit sky. Or towards dawn, the area around Fuji's summit glows pink and its sides radiate a dark purple into what remains of the starlight. The spider had planted himself at an angle on the glass; he sat perfectly motionless, straddling one shoulder of the mountain. I'd never once seen him struggle since the moment I first discovered him trapped there. Impatient, I sometimes snapped a finger on the glass as though to say, 'Hey there!' — sensing, I suppose, that I was losing this test of endurance with him. He couldn't help but stir slightly, having been startled. But that's the only movement he ever made.

About a month later I noticed that he'd lost weight.

'Look, the spider in the toilet has got thinner!'

'So it seems,' my wife said. 'Poor thing.'

'Wonder how long a spider can last without food.'

'I wonder ...,' she said.

She sounded uninterested in the outcome, as though my test was a trivial whim, an imposition on the spider. Somehow I felt resistance to her attitude and told her, 'Well, don't let it get away.'

Another two weeks passed. Now the spider had become noticeably thinner; also, his ashen colour had faded somewhat.

One day, almost two months after I had begun the test and a few days after watching the spider walk over my wall, I heard my wife cry out, 'Oh, dear!' And then, 'it got away.' As usual I was flat on my back, my mind a blank. I thought: She let him get away! Well, what's the difference? So I said nothing.

Careful not to let the spider escape, she always moved both windows together when she cleaned the toilet. But today she absent-mindedly took hold of only one sliding frame. After having opened it half-way, only then did she realise what she'd done. Too late. The speed of the spider's flight astonished her. It was almost as though he'd been eagerly waiting for her to slide open the window. — Such was the gist of my wife's explanation of the incident. I let it go in one ear and out the other, mumbling 'Yes, yes,' and muttering afterwards something to the effect that he was a very lucky devil to survive. The truth is, I had become tired of the endurance contest with the spider. For my money, the matter had been settled, and much the better for that.

*　　*　　*

Over the forty-eight years since the day I was born, the Grim Reaper has been running a three-legged race with me. Not that I've asked for his company, but he has silently accompanied me on my journey through life. These days his image constantly weighs on my mind. Somehow he's assumed a terribly haughty look.

I suppose I was not quite twenty when it first came home to me that I've always had such a preposterous travelling companion. I mean, that's when I began to be aware of life — something that no doubt occurred later to me than to others. I had been too light-hearted to think of such things.

Afflicted with a serious illness when I was twenty-three or

twenty-four, I had almost thrown up my hands in surrender to Death. Somehow I managed to pull through. Since then I suppose he hasn't been too hard to get along with. But I've kept that opinion to myself, for if I let my attitude show, he's bound to get upset. I realise I'll be the loser if I provoke him. It would be irritating, too, to have him quicken the pace on me. But I'm in no mood to write more on this subject .... In a word, though, I have no choice but to go along with Death. The end is the same whether I struggle or not — that much is obvious. All that remains is the question of time.

I wonder if there's anything more insistent and pathetic than man's efforts to escape time and space, his endeavour to grasp whatever he can, be it God or the Absolute or even a straw. However man rationalises, whether saying that an eternity exists in the moment or that the whole exists in the part, his notions are no more than conceptual castles in the sky. Why doesn't man resign himself to his fate? Is it wrong to do so? Incapable of resignation, he rather continues building imposing arrays of fancy solutions. How ingenious and intricate their structure! ... I drowsily contemplate such thoughts, having little choice as I lie in bed gazing at the spiders or flies that now and again appear on my ceiling.

*   *   *

This, too, has to do with bugs. A long time ago I read somewhere about a flea circus and the way the ringmaster trains his fleas. He catches one and puts a small glass bowl over it. The flea hops about on those vaunted legs, but he's surrounded by an impenetrable wall. After having jumped time after time, the flea gets the notion that jumping might possibly be a mistake. He experiments by taking one more leap. Just as he thought: useless. So he gives up and settles down. And then the trainer startles him by tapping on the outside of the bowl. Instinctively, the flea jumps. No good. He cannot escape. The man startles him again. He jumps. He realises it's hopeless. I understand that this conditions the flea to resist jumping no matter what happens. Only then can he learn his tricks and perform.

I recall thinking at the time that this was a terribly cruel method of education. The trainer had, without scruple, reversed something that the flea had been born with. From the viewpoint of the flea, he's forced to realise overnight that he's erred in an act that lies out of his consciousness and, consequently, beyond questioning. It seemed to me that there is no more heartless way to subvert nature than this.

'It's certainly an extraordinary tale,' I said to a young friend who had come in from Tokyo to cheer me up in my sickness. 'Imagine the absolute despair of the flea the moment he realises escape is altogether hopeless! Whether we can imagine what that must feel like, his plight calls for compassion. However, it does appear that the flea is basically a nincompoop, burying his head in the sand and leaving his rump exposed like that .... All the same, I wonder why he doesn't try jumping again — just one more time?'

'He probably thought he's already at the end of his tether,' my friend said with a smile. 'From his point of view, he's already taken his last jump.'

'I wonder ... anyhow, it's a pity,' I said, making a pitiful face.

My friend laughed. 'Here's a story,' he said, 'that recently appeared in print. It contrasts perfectly with the flea's attitude. That whachamacallit, you know, that whatever-you-call-it bee, presumably cannot get off the ground in view of its body weight and the size of its wings. Well, after assembling data on the area of the bee's wings, the number of beats they make per second, and the like, the article said that, physically speaking, this bee could not possibly fly. Actually, however, it flies with no trouble at all. In a word, the article claims that it can fly because it doesn't know it can't.'

'Precisely! That's quite possible — what a great story.' The idea popped into my mind that, in this instance at least, specialists in dynamics were over-confident. More than anything, however, I found it thoroughly amusing that something might be possible simply because one does not realise it is impossible. It was enough to divert me somewhat from the gloomy mood my thoughts about the flea had brought on.

They say one should not overly massage places that pain with neuralgia or rheumatism. When the pain is not too intense, however, having somebody massage you is more often than not enough to get relief. So I have my wife or older daughter give me rub-downs. But if you let the pain get too severe, massaging only makes it worse. Just touching the spot hurts, so at such times there is no way that those looking after me can even touch me. Literally it's 'Hands off!'

When my neuralgia is all right and when I have only to contend with stiff shoulders, one of my affordable 'luxuries' is to snare one of the busy members of my family and get a rub-down. These days my sixteen-year-old daughter stands nearly as tall as her mother, wears the same size Japanese socks, and has become quite strong. Thus, more often than not she massages me. Her fingers are far softer than my wife's, whose hands have become rough from the hard work she's done in the country following our evacuation from Tokyo. That's why my daughter's hands seem more effective. What's more, as I lie on my left side so she can work on my right shoulder, she sometimes reviews her lessons by laying an open book on me as though I were a desk. So massaging me isn't a total waste of time for her.

Sometimes she's talkative. Generally, the topics are commonplace observations about school, about teachers, about friends. I get off with grunting here and there as I listen. But from time to time she asks questions. The other day right out of the blue she asked whether the universe was finite or infinite. I felt as though I'd been rudely awakened from a day-dream.

'Well, I don't suppose anybody knows.'

'Even scholars?'

'Right. I doubt if there's an established theory on it … but it's such a fascinating question I think I'm more interested in the answer than you.' As I spoke I recalled an essay I'd recently read. Some of it came back to me. Scholars estimate the number of spiral nebulae in the universe at about one hundred million; an average distance of two million light years separates these nebulae. The most distant visible nebulae, the ones we might say lie at the edge of the universe, are two hundred and fifty million light years from Earth. And each nebula is twenty-thousand light years in diameter. Thus our own solar system is really nothing but a small component of one nebula among the one hundred million spiral nebulae in the universe. I recalled how I, too, had once lapsed into sentimentality over some such idea as 'the vastness of the universe.' I suppose it happened in the upper grades of middle school when I was around seventeen. Thinking that my sixteen-year-old daughter was now ready for the same experience, I felt moved somehow to show that I supported her wish to learn, so I asked, 'Do you know about light years?'

'Yessir,' she said, expressly answering as though reciting in class. 'A light year is the distance light travels in one year.'

'Excellent,' I said, pretending to be the teacher. 'Well, then, how many kilometers does that amount to?'

'Well ….'

'So, just stop massaging for a minute, get out some paper and a pencil, and work it out.'

'Hmm, let's see, the speed of light per second …,' she said as she multiplied and re-multiplied, turning out figures with thirteen to fourteen digits. 'Golly! The zeroes run right off the page.' When I told her to multiply all that by two hundred and fifty million, she said that such astronomical sums were a pain.

'But this is astronomy, silly!'

'Maybe so, but somehow it takes my breath away and depresses me,' she said, putting down her pencil.

Neither of us said anything for a while. Then I ventured: 'But you know, it doesn't seem to me that you should be astonished at the enormity of the figures because maths is, after all, something man invented and he can set up any units he pleases. Let's suppose that we arbitrarily make one hundred million light years a unit and call it a "super-light year," okay? If we do that, we can describe the radius of the visible universe in terms of two-and-a-half or three super-light years. The figures come to a mere 2.5 or 3 .... On the other hand, if we use more elementary units the zeroes won't just go off the page, they'd be impossible to record even if you spent a lifetime at it.'

'Hmm,' she said, her voice hushed.

'Then the problem comes down to the matter of how you set up your units. If the universe is finite, man's mind can comprehend its size regardless of the number of zeroes involved. And yet, should it be infinite ....'

I didn't finish the sentence because the word 'God' came to mind. My daughter mechanically went on rubbing my shoulder. I felt, however, that the question of man's place in the universe had become an issue for me; it buzzed around in my head as I continued mumbling to myself.

Just where does man fit into the universe anyhow? Exactly where are we hooked into time and space? Is it at all possible that we can on our own discover the answers to such questions? If we could, would we be something more than we are?

I reflect on my experience with the spiders, the flea, and the whachamacallit bee. The two accidentally shut-up spiders were able to escape both times by chance. They had persisted in waiting, still as death, for the opportunity to escape, though they never knew whether it might come. And the dispatch with which they capitalised on the opportunity once it presented itself made me marvel, even though I felt a bit put out by the fact that they got away.

The flea is a nincompoop, he's spineless. The whachamacallit bee has the devil-may-care attitude of a blind man who fears no snake. Even when the impenetrable wall of the bowl has been removed, the flea — who has decided to abandon the possibility of escape — never doubts the wall is still there. The bee makes the impossible possible through 'faith.' I wonder to which type we belong? Or rather, to which do I myself belong?

Personally, I cannot manage the dispassionate and indefatigable deportment of the spider. It would be nice if I could, but I feel it goes against my nature.

And I certainly cannot match the reckless self-confidence of that whatchamacallit bee. Still, can we really call it 'confidence'? If from his point of view he acts unconsciously, confidence isn't in the least bit involved. For the bee, such acts are only natural and so there is little one can say one way or the other about them.

Perhaps I have something in common with the idiotic, spineless flea.

Is there such a thing as being free? Is everything determined? Does someone ordain my 'freedom'? Or is everything a matter of chance? Does an impenetrable wall limit me? I don't know. All I do know is that somewhere along the way my three-legged race with the Grim Reaper will end.

What if some fellow is watching whatever I do the way I observe the spiders, the flea, the bee? And what would I do if some fellow somewhere regulates my every thought and act, the way I myself imprisoned one spider and set another free? What if, like the flea, I have been on the receiving end of someone's cruel educational methods? Haven't I been like one of those bees, with somebody telling me: 'Buddy, you really can't fly'? Has such a being always existed out there, or rather do we invent him? And do we ourselves become what he is? — Nobody can answer these questions.

*   *   *

The flies are bothering me again. It's winter-time now so they only come out during the warmest time of day. Even so, as I lie in bed with the quilt up to my chin, they make my face their playground.

I've made a great discovery about flies. When one alights on my cheek, I chase him away by moving a facial muscle or shaking my head a bit. He flies off, but immediately returns to the same spot. I chase him away again. He flies off and again lands on the same spot. When I do this three times, the fly gives up and does not return to that spot. This happens every single time. If I chase him away three times, apparently it's the nature of every fly to change its mind completely about where it will land.

'It's fun, give it a try,' I tell my family. They only reply non-committally, 'Oh yes, it sounds fun,' but nobody has tried the experiment. They're telling me by their reactions that they're too busy. Of course, I'm not going to compel them to do it. But I have to admit I have been grumbling to myself: 'What does it mean to be that busy? Is being busy so important?'

In addition, I have also managed to accomplish something quite unique: I caught a fly in the wrinkles of my forehead!

A fly had landed on my brow. I responded immediately by lifting my eyebrows, not intending to chase it away. A tumult immediately broke out on my forehead. The wrinkles that were formed when I lifted my eyebrows had securely pinched the fly's legs. I couldn't tell how many had been caught but, stuck in my wrinkles, the fly buzzed vigorously — though in vain. The commotion reminded me of the buzzing a fly makes when you catch one in your hand.

'Hey, come here somebody!' I yelled, not altering the inane look on my face: my eyebrows arched as high as possible to preserve the wrinkles on my forehead. My son, who was now in the first year of junior high school, came in with an expectant look.

'There's a fly on my brow. Get him.'

'How am I going to catch him? I don't think I should hit him with a fly-swatter, should I?'

'Take him with your fingers, quickly. He can't get away.'

My son looked incredulous, but caught him with no trouble.

'How about that? Pretty good, eh? Catching a fly in my wrinkles, that's something. Not everybody can do that. Maybe it's never been done before!'

'Wow, that's amazing,' my son said, trying to wrinkle his forehead and trailing a hand across it to see if he could feel some furrows.

'No way you can do it,' I teased as I watched him passing one hand across his brow as the other carefully held the fly. He was thirteen, big for his age and in the pink of health. He couldn't for the life of him produce a single wrinkle. Those on my forehead were already deep. And not just on my forehead, either.

'What's up? What happened?'

The others came in from the adjoining room. They broke out into gales of laughter on hearing my son's explanation.

'Hey, that is funny!' Even my seven-year-old younger daughter was amused, giving herself up to raucous laughter. As though they had the same thing in mind, each was trying to run a hand over the forehead. When I saw that I said, 'All right, that's enough. Now leave me alone.'

I had begun to feel grouchy.

(January 1948)

8

The Skinny Rooster

— 1 —

The piece for violin and orchestra had just begun on the radio. Ogata was thinking, 'So, *Rondo Capriccioso!*' when his wife came in from the kitchen and abruptly turned it off.

'What's that for?' he asked, less perturbed than perplexed. He could not fathom why his wife had, without warning, acted that way. Dumbfounded, he stared at her. She looked singularly intent.

'If you don't mind, I'd rather not listen to that piece,' she said. Noting that she had assumed a somewhat plaintive look, Ogata thought, 'Well, what's the difference?'

'I don't mind. But what's the problem ...?'

'Music like that depresses me. For some reason it really depresses me.' She hurled the words at him defiantly, over-emphasising the 'really.' Ogata sensed that, like it or not, he would have to do what she wanted.

'OK ... if you want it off, leave it off. I'm not particularly ....'

'I'm sorry,' she said, ready to melt into tears. She turned back into the kitchen to hide her feelings.

Certainly, there had to be some reason for all this. Even so, such eccentric behaviour quite astonished Ogata. Staring intently at the ceiling, he thought hard trying to come up with an explanation, and the fact that he had unexpectedly been given something to think about actually buoyed him up.

In the Ogata — not to mention the average — home, a programme one was enjoying (or at least listening to) did not often get turned off without warning. Of course, in the past, Ogata himself had occasionally turned off some programme or other that was being listened to, but no one complained. Suspecting he had his reasons, his own justification, his family let him have his way. They gave in, for one thing, because Ogata obviously didn't do such things without a reason. For another, they knew he was extremely sensitive to sound and that his illness had aggravated his sensitivity.

Ogata did not imagine that his wife might have felt, 'Well, it's all right for him to lie there day after day while I'm busy rushing about, since he is sick after all. But it's quite a different matter seeing him listening to music in such an obviously nonchalant manner.' Had there been the least hint of that in her attitude, he would not have hesitated to comment. Though not so bright, his wife, in her own way, had managed to spend sixteen or seventeen years with him; now almost thirty-six, she was about the age when a woman learns good judgement in such things. Since by this time she should surely also have mastered most of her husband's quirks, Ogata saw no grounds for her childish intervention. What on earth could have provoked it then? He felt he'd been given a riddle to solve.

While he was getting his thoughts together on the matter, his wife came in silently from the kitchen. She turned the radio back on, saying somewhat timidly, 'I'm sorry about before.'

He had no sooner said, 'That's okay,' than the sound of political rhetoric — someone declaiming in a strangely affected and rather ugly style of speech — abruptly assaulted his ears.

Hastily, Ogata told his wife to turn it off. Now perfectly amenable, his wife broke into a smile and switched off the radio. She then sat beside his bed, as she usually did when taking a break from her household chores.

'The music's already finished,' she said.

'It just used to fill in between programmes. Years ago I used to have a record of it. One of my favourites. It's music for young people.'

'A beautiful melody, isn't it?'

'Then why did you turn it off?' he asked her rather nonchalantly. His wife forced a smile, seemingly reluctant to reply. But Ogata's expression urged her on.

'I couldn't bear listening to it. It was as though ... it was like something beyond ....'

'You mean it was too beautiful?'

'Yes. Somehow it made me sad .... Whenever I hear such music, my miseries just seem utterly ....'

'I see now,' Ogata said. 'I guessed as much.'

'But then I changed my mind. Well, it's not that I changed my mind. I just calmed down. I feel better now.'

'Really?' His response was hardly a response.

He said nothing for a while, thinking only that he had guessed as much. And he felt the unexpected joy of experiencing something a little bit pleasant.

'It's good to let yourself go like that,' Ogata told her. 'You've got to let yourself go now and then. No matter how you look at it, I don't think you can say our life is satisfactory. This is no way to live. Life is supposed to be better than this. I wonder what we dreamed it would be like when we were children. I suppose, though, that we should get upset with present realities instead of dismissing youthful dreams as indulgent fantasies. Life is wretched, shabby, senseless. And today, for you, the violin in *Rondo Capriccioso* suddenly made you see life for what it is, lighting it up for you in an instant. Well, I suppose such things do happen sometimes.'

The moment he finished, Ogata felt sheepish about having let himself get carried away.

'I just couldn't explain how it happened,' his wife said. 'But that's exactly how I feel: "Life is supposed to be better than this." It's not what I dreamed of. I'm just having a nightmare .... Still, you know, I'm not criticising you or my life with you. And I'm not talking only about you or me.'

'You needn't make excuses. I'm not going to. No matter which way you turn, that's the way it is. Aren't we practically in the same boat?'

'I wonder if people can be reborn ....'

'An after-life? Are you asking whether there's life after death?'

'Yes, more or less,' she said.

'I ... well, I have my own way of looking at it. But, whatever it is, at least you can be reborn, so don't worry.'

'If so, that would really be nice. But wouldn't that mean being unkind to you?'

'Not at all. I'm being equally inconsiderate of you, since I'm thinking selfishly of a way to be reborn on a daily basis. But it doesn't seem to be working out too well.'

'Being reborn every day?'

'Why not? I'm not talking about an after-life, but of being reborn hour by hour every day of my life here in this world. But somehow ....'

'Oh, I see what you mean.'

'I mean that you yourself stood on the verge of being reborn a few moments ago.'

'And was I still-born?'

'Well, not quite.'

'Oh, by the way, that reminds me. I hear three kids were born to the Yamamura's goat. Shall I ask for one?'

The abrupt switch momentarily threw Ogata off balance, but he quickly got back into the rhythm of the conversation.

'No good getting a billy goat.'

'So I'll ask for a nanny goat.'

'I wonder if they'll part with a nanny,' he said. 'Besides, if we have one, feeding it could be a problem.'

'If we can milk it every day, feeding it won't amount to much.

We'll be able to manage.'

Our conversation had suddenly switched to Roku, our neighbour's goat. She'd given birth to the kids just the day before, so Ogata's wife said that if they didn't speak up soon for one of them, they would all be gone. She had been preoccupied with ways of getting milk for her ailing husband, which is why she pursued the subject so relentlessly. Her switch in mood had somewhat disarmed him, but Ogata smiled wryly to himself and thought that, for the time being at least, this was the end of the radio episode. She had returned to her usual self.

— 2 —

Ogata had already spent four years flat on his back. His body had given out here and there, but his intercostal neuralgia was particularly painful. Generally speaking, chill and dampness appeared to spark off the neuralgic pains between his ribs. Over-exerting himself had the same effect. Even the slightest movement let Ogata know in no uncertain terms that he was a sick man, so aside from the unavoidable task of writing manuscripts every once in a while, there was little or no work in his daily life. The only parts of his body he put to work, in fact, were hands and mouth, which he could use even in bed. Their functions had shown no signs of deterioration, but nobody needed to tell him that from the waist down he was unrecognisable. He couldn't see his back, but when his wife or eldest daughter scrubbed him in the bath, they called it 'the washboard.' Indeed, the bath-cloth made rub-a-dub sounds as it moved up and down his spine. Once, when Ogata's seven-year-old youngest daughter saw him just after he had got out of the bath, she said, 'Daddy's bottom has gone. He used to have one.'

On another occasion when only partly awake, Ogata heard his wife talking loudly to somebody at the back door: 'Since he can't get any exercise, his legs have become skinnier than ever — like this.' He imagined her joining her thumb and index finger to form a circle. 'It's sad to think that such skinny legs support the whole family.'

It didn't especially upset Ogata that his legs were skinny or that his buttocks had wasted away. But those sudden jabs of neuralgic pain always brought him to his knees. He referred to these attacks as earthquake shocks: violent, severe, strong, or weak. Pains the intensity of a severe 'shock' gave him the feeling that his blood had receded deeply into his chest; his limbs turned to ice, his head to fire. He felt clammy sweat break out all over, but particularly on his forehead and the nape of his neck. He had no choice then but to lie there moaning, curled up in a ball, his arms clasping each other across his chest. He was in such agony that he lacked the strength to thrash about, even had he wanted to. Nor had he the energy to speak.

He experienced an intense sense of pleasure whenever the pain subsided to the level of a strong or a weak 'shock.' His pleasure derived partly from the actual decrease of pain, but he felt far more pleasure in simply being aware that his pain had begun to abate. Whenever the severest pains tapered off, he felt an extraordinary sense of gratitude; it was as though his torments had been unreal.

'It seems ridiculous when you think of it,' he said, 'being overjoyed that my agonies had ended — being free of agonies is the natural condition for healthy people, right? Since being in pain puts a person in such a terribly negative frame of mind, one gets the feeling that he's really gained something when the pain disappears and he gets back to normal. Absurd, isn't it?'

Despite what appeared to be grumbling, Ogata sounded extremely cheerful.

Indeed, experience had taught him that the secret for bearing a given degree of pain lay in increasing the pain threshold. It somehow seemed possible that at the worst point of pain one could participate in some form of religious experience — like the seeker after Truth who chose to court agonies, thereby imposing on himself all sorts of austerities to achieve salvation. That's like saying you had to drown to be saved. However, Ogata dismissed the idea as cockeyed and ludicrous. So far in my life, I've experienced some fairly severe hardships, he thought to himself. And things are no different now. But my style has not been to pursue agonies and afflictions consciously. To date, I haven't even once had the slightest awareness of having pursued them. Rather, I run full tilt to escape them, thinking, 'No thanks, No thanks.' But those awful pains continue to pursue me — impassively and silently, and in a twinkling they catch up. That's the way it's been.

Oh, to have neither pain nor suffering. Wouldn't it be heaven not to need deliverance from such agonies? But no matter. The mere cessation of pain — how wonderful! What on earth have things come to when simply to be free of pain causes such a sense of elation? I can see, he mused, why in their boredom some pleasure-seekers go out of their way to pursue agonies in search of such elation. In perfect health and strong as horses, these characters desire sickness or feign weakness confident that such behaviour will guarantee them peace in the after-life. I want no part of such misguided conduct. — Well, who cares about how others act? At the moment I'm happy ....

Ah, Ogata thought, that reminds me of something that happened a few days ago.

His elder daughter had been massaging his right shoulder because he had felt the onset of a 'shock' somewhere between 'light' and 'slight.' In such cases, taking the precautionary measure of massaging the affected spot usually cleared up the problem with ease. Ogata felt drowsy. Now and then he heard the crinkle of the morning newspaper his daughter had opened over him. Sounds of his wife's singing came from the sink out back. She had been rendering one song after another for some time. He assumed she was doing the laundry because he could hear water splashing between selections.

His daughter, who had been quiet for some time, suddenly said, 'Mum's in a good mood, isn't she?'

'Sounds like it.'

Then they were silent for quite a while and continued listening to her singing — evidently oblivious to everything around her. It was a serene country afternoon, sunlight half-way up the *shōji* door.

After a while, Ogata's daughter said, 'You know, mum told me it really bothered her not to be able to sing when grandma was alive.'

'I know what you mean', Ogata laughed. 'It's a possibility.'

'In those days, she would no sooner start singing away than she would realise with a start that she wasn't supposed to and stop in a fluster. It happened all the time.'

'Poor old mum! How funny! I suppose that's why she's so uninhibited now, singing in full voice like that. But it shows she's in a good mood and it helps her finish her chores. Also she's not getting at you kids, so everybody's happy.' His sixteen-year-old daughter chuckled.

Ogata's wife was singing a selection of schoolgirl favourites from the late 1920s, including hits like *The Gypsies* and *Moonlight on the Castle Ruins*. And by the time she had reached the current hits, such as *Come Back to Sorrento,* she had apparently more or less finished the laundry that the three children had managed so diligently to pile up daily in the hamper. She heaped what she had rinsed into a huge enamelled washbowl and brought it into the yard by the verandah of the eight-mat room where Ogata lay.

'It's an eyesore,' she said, 'but since this is the sunniest spot, here's where the flags of the nation get hoisted.'

'Fine. Hoist away .... Kazuchan, give your mother a hand.'

The girl stopped massaging her father, went over to the verandah, and — no doubt affected by the way her mother had been singing till then — broke out into *Come Back to Sorrento*. Her mother immediately joined in, making a terrific racket at Ogata's bedside.

'Hey! Hey! I'm suffering enough without having you start a

concert on me. Hurry and get the clothes up and do your singing somewhere else.'

'There's no admission charge.'

'You couldn't even pay me to listen.'

'All right then .... Kazuchan, your voice ruins it anyhow. I appreciate your making the effort, but when you join in everything falls apart.'

'But mum, I was perfectly in tune.'

'Even in tune, you still have that zoo-prano ....'

Ever since she was a little girl, Ogata's eldest daughter frequently burst out with hyena-like giggles. With a voice like that, they told her, she would never be a soprano but a zoo-prano.

So the women stopped singing. They quickly hung up the washing under the eaves of Ogata's room, and his daughter came over again to work on his shoulder. Shadows from the flags of the nations danced over the *shōji*.

That was the scene that had floated into Ogata's mind. He recalled it with a warm feeling, thinking that his wife was undoubtedly at her best at times like that. She took the dirty clothes the children were continuously accumulating and scrubbed and rubbed away at them without getting in the least bit bored — utterly absorbed in the most meaninglessly repetitive chores, yet her uninhibited singing revealing her peace of mind. Ogata likened it to a case of perfect combustion without a trace of smoke. When she was like that, it made no difference to her whether she found the work meaningful or not. Unfortunately, Ogata thought, for me, ah, for me, bliss is never a gift.

— 3 —

Even someone as carefree as Ogata's wife experienced those rare occasions when sudden fits of revulsion and disgust for — or, more bluntly, of despair over — the realities of her everyday existence cropped up. The incident at the outset of this story, which describes her turning off the radio, serves as an example of how these fits manifest themselves.

But let's return to Ogata, a man of fifty who has been sickly all his life, a fellow who writes stories and is at the moment a complete invalid.

Ogata Shōkichi is a nondescript family man. From an outsider's point of view, he isn't all that bad a husband, nor a horrid father ... anyway, that's how he thinks people see him.

When Ogata was around twenty years old, he had a confrontation with his late father, who at that time was exactly Ogata's present age. They were at loggerheads over the contrasting ways they looked at life and how to make a living. One could say in a word that their argument concerned the philosophy of life, but because Ogata wouldn't be happy with such a term, let's leave it vague. Since his father died on his sick-bed during the height of the feud, Ogata suddenly found himself liberated from the confrontation without having had to struggle. He immediately enrolled in the Tokyo school that he had till then refrained from entering in deference to his father's stern injunctions. And shortly thereafter, having arrived at conscription age, he had his draft examination and was designated Class II-B, student reservist. As a result of his experiences over those three or four months, he felt he had suddenly grown up. Aided to a great extent by the indigenous ethos that had trained him since childhood to take, as the successor, a rank in the family second only to his father, he found it easy to settle down into being a proper head of the house. Even while his father was alive, neither his two younger brothers nor his two younger sisters, nor even his mother, could stand up to him; so it was quite natural that things happened as they did.

Thus evolved this young head of the house who was excessively arbitrary, but for all that, quite tolerant and what you could call self-complacently perceptive. His arbitrariness derived from his habit of never tolerating interference from anyone once he had determined to act. It was not a matter of being impervious to reason, for up to the point of making a decision on some matter he pondered and considered the views of others. But once he had decided, he never wavered. His tolerance arose naturally out of the way he doggedly held his ground. Thus he always had a smile on his face; he could afford to smile because he generally got his way. He was a good son, a good brother, and friends at college considered him an interesting and agreeable fellow.

By the time he was ready to graduate, however, Ogata Shōkichi rarely smiled anymore. For one thing, he had squandered most of the resources his father had left the family. You see, he had quite unscrupulously squandered three to four times the amount of money that the average college student needed to live on in Tokyo. On top of that, his brothers and sisters, though not spendthrifts, were also at school. There was no doubt that a crisis loomed large for the Ogatas — a family that neither toiled nor reaped. Thanks to the 1923 Kanto earthquake, that crisis arrived far earlier than Ogata had anticipated.

He had never earned a single *sen*, nor had his mother nor any of his brothers or sisters. They were all inept at keeping accounts — the very reason that when they saw the coffer drained their first response was not to consider rational ways of dealing with the problem but to become surly. The money they had been spending so nonchalantly unexpectedly turned the tables and began maliciously to haunt them. Once aware of what had happened, they became flustered, disheartened, and edgy. And they all looked to Shōkichi, the head of the house: 'Just who's to blame for this?'

At least that's the question Ogata perceived beneath his family's abashed glances. He consciously braced himself and thought, 'They're right.' If it was a matter of responsibility, then it all fell on him. He could not shift a single particle of blame onto them. Don't panic, he thought. For better or for worse, I'll manage .... Ogata naturally assumed this stance as a matter of principle. Beyond that, however, it reflected his disposition, rooted perhaps in the radical way he had been raised to be the heir. He was quite enamoured of the idea, 'Leave it to me.' (It may have been around then that he saw Harold Lloyd perform in the movie farce called *The Freshman*. The film featured a hero played by Lloyd who was always saying. 'Leave it to me.' He was a charmingly affable busybody who made everybody laugh at him by butting in on the flimsiest of pretexts, floundering around, getting into trouble, and then botching up the job beautifully. In the film, the hero manages by some fluke — in a way typical of American comedy — to get himself out of the mess. Ogata noticed a sour smile creeping over his lips as he watched it.) Mark you, even at fifty, he was hardly a reformed character! Sometime before, with great amusement, he had told his wife about this movie, probably after he'd been in a similar predicament. She had said, 'I wish I could have seen it.' Ever since then she would occasionally jeer at Ogata's behaviour with, 'Hey! you're playing *The Freshman* again.'

Behaving like the person in charge gave Ogata a sense of manfulness. Thus, he inwardly assumed the quixotic attitude, 'Leave it to me,' and floundered around like Lloyd. But he differed from Lloyd in that he could not by some fluke manage to get himself out of a mess. Consequently, his family lost confidence in him.

Loss of confidence was a heavy blow to a man of Ogata's disposition. He was by nature the cocky rooster, not the hen. He had little inclination to 'be loved,' but he rather liked people having to depend on him. 'Being loved' seemed tacky to him, so he was not one to welcome something like that even when it involved a woman. He would be satisfied to love her (if she were one he loved) in his own way; he asked only that she depend on him. (That's why he found an idea like 'democratic love' rather hard to take. Regardless of the incident, that's how it was with every single woman he'd ever had any dealings with. Relationships worked out fine if they followed this formula. If they didn't, the relationship never got off the ground — and this wasn't the case only in love affairs, either. Ogata always believed that this personal disposition to play the destitute but demanding *samurai*, the head of the house barely able to keep his head above water, had derived from heredity and environment. And so at this late date there was no way he could deny his nature.)

Ogata had destroyed his family's esteem for him. He had lost what had helped him hold out till then. In his case, he believed that if the family could not accept his arbitrariness, then neither could he be magnanimous with them. Once he wrote to his mother from the house of some woman in Tokyo where he had ensconced himself: 'From now on I'm going to be a villain!' After that, he burned every letter that came from home, one after the other, without opening a single one. (A novelist friend once modelled a character in a short story on the Ogata of those days. In one passage the hero flushes an unopened letter from his mother down the lavatory. Although fiction, Ogata found that repulsive. When he read the story in a magazine, he wasted no time telling his friend that even if the letter had not come from his mother, there was no way he could ever flush it down the lavatory. Nor had he ever considered such an act. Since the two were on good terms, the incident passed with strained laughter and smiles. However, when Ogata reflected on the fact that during their long friendship this had been the only time he had registered the slightest protest with this friend, he actually found himself smiling at his old-fashioned sensibilities. When the story later appeared in an anthology of his friend's writings, Ogata found the passage had been rewritten to take account of his criticisms.)

Ogata had become an incorrigible son, a scandalous brother, and the scourge of his relatives.

He had practically given away family lands that had been passed down from generation to generation, thus incurring the icy sneers of the townsfolk. He received a card from his mother telling him, 'I'll die if you act like that,' but it didn't appear to bother him in the slightest. From time to time he got together with one of his sisters when she was in her last year at a woman's college, but when she once made it a point to say in a letter, 'I wish you'd be the brother you once were,' he barely flinched. He just calmly went out drinking.

When it came to drinking, none of his friends could top him. He often picked fights when he drank but made it a point never to start anything with people he knew. He challenged only strangers. There were absolutely no psychological complications in his behaviour; it was only a game with him. Since he didn't know his adversary, he could hardly ascertain the extent of the peril ahead of him, which, in turn, made the game more thrilling.

The woman he had married, after prevailing upon his mother for her consent, kept saying that love should be this or that, so he gradually lost interest in her. Beyond that, she went so far as to complain that Ogata didn't do an ounce of work. That ruined everything. For the first time in his life, he struck a woman.

One night Ogata hit her and she cried herself to sleep. He discovered some dried blood on her left ear when she woke the next morning.

He sent her to the doctor. Soon she returned bandaged from her jaws to the top of her head and from her forehead to the back of her head in what looked, from the side, like an 'X.' She claimed she had a ruptured eardrum.

A graduate from a smart Tokyo girls' school who had recently opened a coffee shop, this woman who was his wife loved to dress smartly. She was twenty-five or twenty-six years old, the widow of an army captain whose estate allowed her to open the shop. Her sister, aged about twenty-one and the graduate of an even better school, worked with her; the two of them had hired a maid and business was very good indeed.

Regular customers included many students and professors at Ogata's college. Most of them knew him. Some had told his wife, 'You look rather attractive in bandages.' 'Really?' she said, smiling sweetly as she ran the fingers that were her pride and joy over the bandage.

Staring intently into the mirror at her carefully-applied make-up, she tried to find the most effective way to put on the bright white bandage. She arranged her black wavy hair to match. And then, tossing the mirror a sweet smile, she turned to Ogata and asked, 'How's this?'

'Looks great,' he said, as though expecting the question. Then he looked away. — Just what the devil does she think that bandage is for, anyway? Does she imagine I'd hit a woman without cause? He concluded, for no particular reason, that there was no room for the likes of him in this world.

Shortly after, Ogata left her and without notice headed for a city near Hiroshima. He did not inform his family about where he had gone.

An author whom Ogata had respected for many years lived in that quaint city snuggled against a mountain. It was precisely because of this esteemed writer that Ogata — a creaky vessel ready to go under and with no other port to put in at — barely limped into Onomichi, the only haven left.

He rented a small house near the man he venerated and lived

in it for some eight months. For a number of years Ogata had wanted to write just one piece like the stories this man wrote. He had laboured long and hard to achieve that goal, but the more he exerted himself the stiffer his shoulders became. As a result, he ended up unable to write a single thing for four or five years. Living in Onomichi for eight months brought home to him the simple truism: a crow trying to imitate a cormorant will drown. Out of his profound sense of resignation there arose, little by little, the refreshing idea that a duck differs from a swan. A duck should act like a duck and try continually to discover what it means to be a duck.

More or less able to face things, Ogata returned to Tokyo. There he settled accounts with the woman as he had planned and made a fresh start. About six months later he became acquainted with Yoshiye, his present wife. That spring Yoshiye had graduated from a girls' school in her home province and shortly after had come to visit a married classmate living in Tokyo.

It so happened that her friend's husband was one of Ogata's younger acquaintances.

Cut off from his hometown and having dissolved his marriage, Ogata resembled a vagabond. Going over to visit his friend from time to time gave him the opportunity to get acquainted with Yoshiye. After two months of vacillating, he made up his mind.

More than anything else, he had been struck by Yoshiye's trusting naïvete. A lively, unsullied eighteen-year-old, she stood five feet two, weighed just about 100 pounds and had been an athlete at school. But these qualities alone could hardly have attracted Ogata. The fact was, he had already begun to turn into something of a sober 'duck.' At long last, he had set about disposing of the self-indulgent 'I'm a superfluous man syndrome' that had lured him into acting the self-styled rogue. He was already thirty.

— 4 —

Because of her youth and lack of experience, Yoshiye had an unadulterated air about her. Owing perhaps to her upbringing, she had managed to preserve much of her childish innocence. Each meeting with her had a cathartic effect on Ogata, a man polluted by bad company and worldliness. At least once a day she made him burst out laughing. Yoshiye would ask him earnestly, 'Why are you laughing? What's so funny?' And he would say, 'Sometimes I laugh at nothing in particular. It's one of my quirks.' He'd been so touched on several occasions that tears came to his eyes — and he took himself to task for getting emotional at his age. I shouldn't be treating her this way, he thought; I shouldn't make fun of her.

Ogata found the opportunity to show just what sort of rooster he was. It happened on one occasion when Yoshiye was imagining she was riding on something like a luxury liner. In fact, the craft was just a beaten-up old junk. The slightest wave or the slightest breeze made it creak, ship water, and roll dangerously. The happy-go-lucky passenger knew nothing of these defects; she only said, 'What gorgeous clouds!' 'O, seagulls!' 'Isn't the ocean nice?' The captain, beside himself with panic, screwed up enough courage to say, 'Certainly.'

Gradually, seventeen years went by. Even somebody as simple as Ogata's wife had discovered along the way that she was not really on a luxury liner. And she knew she was no longer the sole passenger, either. Three children had come aboard. In a story written some dozen years earlier, Ogata had said, 'Eventually this naïve woman will become a seasoned spouse too crafty to deal with. It's a dreary thought, but that's life.' Granted, things hadn't yet come to that, but Yoshiye had been moving in that direction. It certainly was a dreary thought. Nevertheless, had she not changed, the old junk with its extra passengers would have bellied over long ago.

During his lengthy convalescence, Ogata frequently tried to untangle this web of thought, wondering why he wanted to have her both changed and not changed.

Yoshiye's tendency to be what he labelled a fat-head or a dope had definitely decreased considerably with maturity. Since they were inbred characteristics, they surfaced from time to time. When they did, Ogata reproached her with, 'I'll write that up on you!' At the same time, however, he found himself attracted by her pristine naturalness. Compared to other women her age, Yoshiye's behaviour to this day — regardless of how you interpret it — contains many elements of impracticality and surely flies in the face of convention.

For a time after they got married, Ogata viewed with suspicion Yoshiye's somewhat excessive impracticality and lack of common sense. He suspected they were manifestations of that indiscriminate fawning or coquettishness that young girls so frequently affect. With that in mind, Ogata once chided her, 'Acting like that — is insincere.' He gradually came to realise, however, that she was not a phony. She was a bit of a headache, yes, but at least she had the fascination of nature itself.

A man like Ogata — so obsessed with writing that he kept at it doggedly despite his lack of success — no doubt seemed to the average person in society an impractical chap who flew in the face of convention. He was well aware of this and made it a point to behave as much as possible in a practical and conventional manner. He did so, first of all, because it was difficult for him to see himself

as a genius or even out of the ordinary. Further, because he knew
he was neither a genius nor out of the ordinary he concluded it would
be a mistake, and shameful as well, to act as though he were.

Such thoughts made him something of a stoic. Ogata's feudal
paternalism and rooster psychology harmonised marvellously with
his stoicism, making it appear as though he more or less knew what
he was doing.

But that's not the way it really was. He had squandered his
family's resources. He had as good as broken off all relations with
the rest of the family. He had impulsively rejected the woman he
had arbitrarily married. And as he drifted around like a stray dog
he had thrown in his lot with a girl he knew nothing about. He was,
as it were, in a mess. And nothing had gone the way he had hoped
it would. His decision to marry Yoshiye had been considerably
influenced by the desire to use remarriage as an opportunity to make
a fresh start. He had told himself, 'Well, it's about time.'

For a number of years he had been fond of the expression,
'When you're weary, rest. The others won't get too far ahead' —
something a Russian author had said. He admired this passage, which
only an extremely sensitive person with some depth could have
uttered. Now that Ogata had turned thirty-two, however, he looked
around and was unprepared to find that the others were quite far
ahead of him. It rekindled his sense of exasperation to discover that
he had rested too long.

Ogata tacked a poem on that subject to the water-stained wall
of the place they had moved into after their marriage — a shabby,
totally barren 9 x 12-foot room they had rented in a boarding house.
Yoshiye recited the poem loudly, the way children read their lessons
in class: "The wintry wind / A single path / Stretching far ...." Is
that a *haiku?*'

'That's what I intended.'

'You *intended?* So, it's one of Mr Ogata's works.'

'Works? ... Well, hardly what you could call a *work.*'

'That sounds like a *haiku* I learned in school. You know, Bashō's
"This path / No others travel / Late in autumn."'

'Hmmm, it does?' Ogata reddened, a bit flustered. He continued
testily, 'But they're different. In Bashō's poem there's quite an air
of self-importance. The idea "I travel alone" bursts with the pride
and assertiveness of one without peers. Mine isn't like that at all.
It's late in the day. A long road lies ahead of me, yet I must drag
myself on despite the fact that others have already outdistanced me
— that's the pathos of my verse. But as a poem, friend Bashō's seems
better.'

'Friend Bashō's ...'? Yoshiye gurgled raucously. It seemed she would never stop laughing. Ogata imagined that his sour analysis had been really ill-timed.

All things considered, he had not strayed very far out of line during the seventeen years since that event. Not that Ogata never acted indiscreetly, but he managed to nip indiscretions in the bud before they developed into anything serious. One might say that this indicates the extent to which he was determined to make a go of it. In effect, however, to a large extent his wife's behaviour had unpremeditatively led him to walk the straight and narrow. It was like the two boozers at a bar. The one who got drunk first was better off, for the sober one had to look after him and see that he got home. In any contest of whooping it up or letting oneself go, Ogata had already ascertained that constitutionally he was no match for this woman. If he got to doing what he felt like and imitated her, their life would have been a mess in no time. As a matter of course, then, their relationship became one where Yoshiye was the float, Ogata the sinker.

— 5 —

But Ogata had begun to think that even the sinker-float combination in his family had apparently gone through a transformation after he became ill. In a word, his wife's attitude to life had become quite hard-headed. It is easy to see why.

She had matured and, moreover, had become the mother of three children under sixteen. After living in Tokyo since their marriage, they suddenly found themselves living in the countryside. Worse, still, they were living in her husband's native village where she was not at all familiar with local customs, conventions, or anything. After her mother-in-law passed away, she had to deal with people directly. Most important, Ogata was ill and one simply didn't know how long he would last.

He had been moved to reminisce about the contrasts between past and present, picturing in his mind how, in the past, his wife had been such a scatter-brain and rather simple-minded and thinking that (surprise of surprises!) she could, after all, manage to respect convention when she made the effort. There were aspects of her unusual conventional behaviour which slightly amused and somewhat impressed him.

Once, to see how she would react, he said to her, 'So you've become the "Perfect wife and wise mother!"'

'Who?'

'You, of course.'

'But what else? Well, isn't this what one is supposed to be!'

Ogata only vaguely smiled. Actually, he felt as though he had lost something. The shrewd, hard-boiled person, male or female, whose practicality left nothing to be desired held no fascination for him. Such people were hard to get along with and he felt ill at ease with them. They were, in a word, uninteresting. He also found it altogether depressing to contemplate the prospect that his wife — a person he must face every day, year in and year out, till the day he died — would be the 'Perfect wife and wise mother.'

If this trend continued, he feared she might really turn into an ordinary conventional woman. But really, that could never happen because her present behaviour, just a make-shift veneer, was not at all rooted in her character. 'My illness has shocked her into it; it's only a temporary phenomenon. Yes, that's it .... ' Thus Ogata concocted ways to assuage his fears that Yoshiye had lost something of her old self.

On the one hand, she could still sing with much gusto while doing the laundry — despite being too old for that sort of thing — unconcerned about what people might think. But on the other hand, she arbitrarily turned off the music her husband was enjoying merely because she couldn't bear to hear such sublime melodies. Well, Ogata had finally come to terms with his wife's spontaneity and foolhardy approach to life, although he would never tell her that. There's still hope for me, he thought.

Ogata viewed his wife's attitude as a reflection of his own, thus bringing the problem back to himself. Because she cannot be sure how long I'll last, she can no longer look to me for everything. And, though out of character, she persists in her new rôle. I'm unable to discharge my responsibilities, but if she cannot be the way she was in the old days — acting as though she is on a luxury liner and, without a second thought, saying exactly what is on her mind — that doesn't augur well for me, Ogata thought. If she eventually loses her immaturity and her obliviousness to the so-called real world, her dreams and aspirations, and if she turns into a realist who thinks that being practical is the be-all-and-end-all ... well, that will be the day for me to throw in the towel.

Watching the chickens next door, it occurred to Ogata how much the rooster acts like a rooster, the hens like hens, the chicks like chicks. Of course, that's exactly what everybody expects of chickens, but one thing in particular impressed him. As the rooster calmly tended his brood of hens, a crow suddenly flew low over them. The faint whirr of wings and a huge shadow swept over the chickens. At once the rooster set up a clamorous alarm and assumed a defensive stance, his eyes darting in all directions. The hens nestled close to him, the chicks scampered nimbly under their mothers'

wings and made not a sound. In the way they had grouped together
not a single feather was out of place.

When it became clear that nothing would happen, they broke
formation and returned to their feeding. Ogata perceived a touch of
the ludicrous in the pose the rooster had assumed. What was there
for him to get so upset about? Wasn't it just the whirr of wings and
the shadow of a crow? Worse, his fighting posture seemed a bit
ridiculous. Ogata thought nevertheless that anyone observing his
behaviour might perhaps find it equally ridiculous.

— 6 —

Thus Ogata found himself acting more kindly towards the members
of his family. In part, he had consciously chosen to act that way. In
part, it had become natural for him to do so. (His kindliness was
not limited to family members, nor did he direct his new-found
considerateness to people alone. He tended to act more reasonably
towards everything other than himself, towards everything that
touched his senses, that touched his heart.)

Ogata always wanted his family to be joyful rather than angry,
laugh rather than cry, be cheerful rather than depressed. In fact, he
wished only for their happiness.

Even if this change in him may not have been especially
remarkable, it apparently affected those around him to a considerable
extent. Note, for example, the following confidential exchange
between his elder daughter and his wife:

'Daddy's less irritable these days.'

'I hadn't actually thought about it,' Mrs Ogata said. 'I suppose
he is.'

'He's not as sick as he was. I'm sure of that.'

'Maybe he doesn't have the energy any more to get upset.'

'Mum, don't say things like that!'

Nobody knew how long it would take Ogata to recover. Still,
his family did not seem to get tired of acting as nurse-maid for so
many years. He realised that they were intensely aware they would
be in sad straits should they let him die, so one way or another they
were determined to keep him alive. If only because he was the
bread-winner, all other considerations aside, you might say it was
natural to hope for his survival. When all is said and done, they
obviously had every reason to want him to pull through no matter
what it cost them. 'When daddy gets well ....' 'When daddy recovers
....' With eyes glistening, whenever they talked of their hopes or
aspirations for the future, they prefaced their remarks with the
concern that father might recover. Keiko, the younger girl,

exemplified their hopefulness. For three years she had been asking him, 'Daddy, when you're well, we'll go to the beach at Kōzu, won't we? Just me and you.' And this summer once again her mother, big sister, or big brother had often taken her swimming at Ōiso and Kōzu, but she was never able to go with her father. Another summer had ended. The day before school began she said, 'Daddy, will you be well next year? You will, won't you?'

'Next year? Of course, by then I'll be up and about again.'

'Next summer we'll go swimming at Kōzu. Just daddy and me.'

'Oh, you bet. To Ōiso and Odawara, too. Just the two of us.'

'Great!' Keiko beamed dreamily, a look he sometimes saw on her face as she slept. However could such a simple thought like going with her father to the beach at Kōzu make this little rascal so happy? It could be that perhaps her every last tender hope and dream for her ailing father had been condensed into that very simple thought.

Ogata sighed to himself: 'Honestly, this ties me hand and foot — I can't very well die even if I want to.' On the other hand, he felt quite aware at that moment of how his daughter's words tickled the old rooster in him. He even felt a bit cocky. 'Good,' he thought. 'I'll get well, and even if I don't they can at least rest assured that I do not intend to go without a fight.' He imagined that the defiant look in his eyes may have resembled the way his neighbour's rooster reacted to the crow.

Actually, there is another important reason why Ogata became more considerate towards others. He had consciously created within himself a small cell that he kept secret from everyone.

Not even his family knew of this cell despite the fact that he spoke to all of them every day and each member of his household knew at a glance more or less how the others felt. They were not likely to be aware of his secret, even without his trying to keep it from them, because it had no relation to their concerns and represented something they had probably never seen, heard about, or considered.

For all his efforts at concealment, this was by no means an easy matter. Anyone in Ogata's circumstances would no doubt understand immediately. In a nutshell, the same doubts generally plague all people in ill health. They wonder, Why was I born? Why am I alive? Why must I die? As they consider these questions, moreover, sick people become impatient for answers. Endless doubts constantly boil up in their minds. From ancient times to the present day, it is almost as though man has concentrated his total energies on finding answers to these questions; and now he can hardly bear the weight of the ideas he has amassed. His efforts to find answers have spawned the gigantic accumulation of information in the fields of religion, philosophy, science, and the arts. Ogata had been taught, he couldn't remember when, to look at life in this way and so imagined that this was the nature of knowledge. But from the perspective of his present predicament, none of the information generated by these fields of knowledge was relevant.

Like normal people, Ogata had no idea what pain was until it had dug its nails into him. Nor did he much care to do the digging himself. He had more or less learned all about pain through books and conversation, and at times he himself had lots to say about it when he wrote or talked with people. But that's all it ever amounted to. He hadn't actually experienced it.

Ogata felt pain for the first time when he became ill and hit the truth head on — realising that, no matter how he looked at it, he was not going to live much longer. At this point, the obvious no longer seemed so obvious. When he looked again at things he had previously ignored, he found them intensely fresh. And when he focused his attention on even the most ordinary items around him, he no longer found them so ordinary. Ensconced in his hidden cell, he painstakingly set about breaking everything down and trying to make sense of it. At those moments he was completely isolated, utterly oblivious even to all the members of his family around him.

He knew the futility of informing anyone in his family about what was going on in his cell. There was no reason to expect that he could possibly explain it to those so naïve, so young, so full of life. After all, he thought, it's obvious that it wouldn't make sense to them — there would be something wrong if it did. Full of life, they must weep and laugh and sing. These twilight thoughts of a wreck like Ogata could only undermine their joy of life. In good time they, too, will experience the inescapable evening of life. Far better to leave such matters till then.

Thus Ogata continued to interact with his family without letting on that anything had changed in him. Despite the fact that he was never remiss in the way he spoke or dealt with them face to face, his mind was almost completely dominated by thoughts that had no relation to his dealings with them. He imagined himself an insensitive and cruel creature. But if he didn't give any thought to his life, who on earth would do it for him? He was both grateful for and heartened by the care he received from his family, their nursing of him, their devoted efforts to save or prolong his life. But still, he thought, that's an entirely different matter. Ogata merely hoped to make sense of his life, his existence — that and nothing else, an extremely straight-forward hope. And he had no choice but to make sense out of it on his own. He could only confront the task as a single individual, he could only do so by himself, alone.

One day a message had arrived from a young literary critic. His note closed with the words, 'The baby is crying, my wife is in a huff, and I've got a mountain of chores piling up — so these days I really wish I could become a Buddhist priest and flee the world.' In answer Ogata wrote, 'If it's just a matter of fleeing your family and society, you can do that much right at home. Why not give it a try?' He had written without having given these words much thought, but several days later it occurred to him, 'That is the answer!' Given Ogata's circumstances, you might say that his answer perfectly described what had happened to him. Of course, he hadn't settled down into an Eastern-style commitment to the transience of life or resignation to the inevitable. Had that been the case, he probably would not have bothered writing a single line. Nor would there likely have been the need to. Ambition and passion still survived in him.

Simply to prepare himself a private cell to which he alone had access and, with leisure time on his hands (in every sense of the word he was quite the man of leisure), to withdraw from his family and hole up in his cell — that might well be one way to become a Buddhist priest and flee society.

'Hmm, perhaps this is "The Art of Taking the Tonsure and Fleeing Society by Doing Nothing"! Alas, the rooster in me is only a shadow of what he once was. It looks as though more eggs have been laid in the chicken-coop next door. No way can I match that rooster's vigour. But how about the way he struts around ready to fight without a hint of indecision? A splendid, an impressive show. Dismissing it as ludicrous reminds me of somebody singing a ditty on his way to the block. I'll not fly off the handle but hold my ground. I'll hold my ground level-headedly — keeping a stiff upper lip and swallowing my pride — till my present miseries end, whenever that happens. Yes, that's the course I must take.'

(APRIL 1949)

9
Day of the Nuptials

— 1 —

As the day of his daughter's wedding approached, Ogata became unaccountably edgy.

He knew little about the conventions of marriage. He and his wife had managed to get married without following any of the customary formalities. They had consulted no one. They had asked nobody for help. During the twenty-five years since, not a single marital problem had cropped up, so naturally they paid no attention to the institutions of matrimony in Japan.

But things were different with their first daughter, Hatsuye. To begin with, the Ogatas had received a proposal from a third party asking whether they were interested in having their daughter marry into such-and-such a family. The Ogatas had absolutely no knowledge of the family or the young man in question.

Nor had that been the first request for Hatsuye's hand. A proposal had come while she was still at college, but Ogata rejected it without informing his daughter. And, following a family conference, he vetoed a proposal received immediately after her graduation on the grounds that it was still too early for marriage.

But Ogata, his wife, and Hatsuye as well had to give some thought to the present proposal. After all, his daughter had already turned twenty-three.

Ogata was the least enthusiastic about seeing Hatsuye married. In short, he felt that since he had to marry her off he would prefer to postpone it as long as possible. He had no specific reasons. He simply wanted to part with her later rather than sooner.

After a careful inquiry, the prospective groom's family seemed well off. A father, a mother, a son. Ogata found that the father stayed in a large provincial city where he headed the branch office of a big concern. The son lived in Tokyo where he worked for a different company. The mother busily travelled back and forth between husband and son.

'So that's why they want to find a wife for him soon,' Ogata said knowingly.

The father had graduated from Hitotsubashi Commercial University, a famous national college, and now worked in a brokerage firm; the son had attended the same private college from which Ogata graduated. But having majored in the sciences, he worked for a manufacturing company. The world these people inhabited differed utterly from the world of a man who writes stories. But for that very reason, Ogata sensed that it would probably be easy to get along with them.

'Well,' he said to Hatsuye, 'how about meeting him?'

'Fine.'

'And then date him for a while?'

'I'd like that.'

The cheerless thought occurred to Ogata that, if she was going to meet him and date him, she was as good as gone.

The young man came to meet the Ogatas accompanied by the person who had delivered the proposal. The boy was tall, well built, and healthy — a cheerful fellow. 'I'm twenty-eight,' he said.

The young man and Hatsuye went out together about once or twice a month. Each time she returned with a detailed report.

This continued through the spring into summer. The other family then began pressing the Ogatas for a decision. Ogata's wife was the most interested in making a positive response. Ogata was indecisive, yet he found no reason for opposing the match.

'Hatsuye has the most at stake,' he said. 'What does she think about it?'

'She doesn't mind.'

'Well, then, I suppose it's okay,' Ogata said, with a hint of submission in his voice.

It was about midsummer when the families exchanged engagement presents. Ogata found it rather amusing that such a convention had appeared in his home. On the other hand, it alarmed him — even as he wondered what there was to be alarmed about — to think that once he had gone this far there could be no turning back.

The other family sent word that they would like the ceremony in the autumn — in October or November.

Ogata's wife appeared happy enough with that.

But then he said, 'Let's make it next spring.'

'By postponing it, you'll only make it harder on yourself.'

'But we can't make the arrangements at such short notice.'

'What arrangements? Certainly we don't need to do anything especially elaborate ....'

'That's true,' Ogata said. 'But I would rather not have to rush about. It's very tiring.'

'Tiring' — Ogata's trump card. He had a weak constitution.

That's why he detested being forced to change pace. Ogata had somehow managed to survive the dozen or so years since the end of the Pacific War solely because of a stubborn insistence on maintaining his own pace. Well aware of this, his wife couldn't say much in reply.

They decided to have the ceremony around the middle of March in the coming year. 'There is at least six months till then,' Ogata thought, glancing across the room at his daughter, busily involved in something.

— 2 —

It took two hours by train to Tokyo from where Ogata lived in the Shōnan countryside. He often went there for business or pleasure. In the past, he always stayed overnight at an inn — it being too taxing to make the round trip in one day.

Nowadays, however, he could manage. Though he had regained some of his old strength, the trip tired him nevertheless. He would leave home in the morning, and by the time he finished his business and boarded the train at Shinbashi or Tokyo in the evening — or later at night — he was ready to collapse into his seat from fatigue.

One day he noted a bouquet in the luggage rack above him. He had stretched out on his side over the double seat. With the nosegay visible in the corner of his eye, he thought about the newlyweds who had either forgotten or discarded it.

The reserved coach had just returned from the run to Atami. Ogata waited on the platform and boarded as the Tokyo-bound passengers got off. He didn't have to stand there till workers finished sweeping out the cars.

In the rush to get to the inn the newlyweds had probably forgotten all about the bouquet on the rack. It had returned alone to the Tokyo station from which it had departed. That was Ogata's first thought. But later he thought that, no, maybe they hadn't forgotten it after all. Perhaps they meant to leave it — too shy to carry an attention-getting bouquet into the station at Atami. He smiled wryly, his eye still on the luggage rack, thinking, 'Six of one, half a dozen of the other.'

Several newlyweds had boarded the same coach. Since the train was bound for Atami, they could be headed there, or for either Yugawara or Hakone. Some couples had bouquets, some did not. Some were talking light-heartedly, others just sat stiffly silent.

The train arrived at the station where Ogata had to change. Taking his small parcel from the rack, he glanced at the bouquet. Its carnations, chrysanthemums, gerberas and whatever seemed slightly wilted. As he headed for the platform to catch the local, he thought it would be nice to put the bouquet in a vase when he got home.

— 3 —

Ogata lacked confidence in everything. If it was true of his work, it was even truer of day-to-day worldly affairs.

In his youth, Ogata had ventured into literature against his father's wishes. He hadn't the slighest idea of what he was getting into. That explains why he not only became estranged from his family but was held in contempt by those who knew him. Inexperienced in the ways of the world, he did whatever he pleased with a wreckless disregard. As a result he went through all the family resources, upset his family, and caused aggravation to his friends. In his twenties he took a wife but before long left her.

He was keenly aware that he had indeed been a difficult individual — unaware of his limitations. But it was too late to turn back. Even now, half-way through his fifties, Ogata still lacked self-confidence. He had become resigned to the fact that there was nothing he could do about the way his sense of inadequacy increased over the years. Rather, he felt amazed that he had managed to survive so long.

Quite set in his ways, Ogata had excessively clear likes and dislikes. He never bothered with anything that failed to interest him. His own interpretation of such behaviour held that it, too, stemmed from his lack of self-confidence. You can't say he never gave the impression of being brash, but it was really no more than unpremeditated resistance to whatever hemmed him in.

Resistance. In his case that meant being passive. Everyone else might be active. He was not. That was his way of resisting.

— 4 —

Ogata was thirty-one at Hatsuye's birth. He had married his present wife the year before and they had begun their married life in one room in a dingy boarding house on the seedy outskirts of Tokyo. Compared to how others lived, theirs was a miserable existence. But because he supposed he deserved no better, Ogata found it rather easy to put up with his miseries. He had made his bed and now must lie on it — deep down, that was how he felt. Still, it was too bad for Yoshiye — his eighteen-year-old wife who had come to share his lot. Naturally, Ogata's attitude to her was partly that of a husband and partly that of a father. And Yoshiye's personal sentiments in the matter encouraged him to treat her that way, for she had lost her father when she was very young.

One month before Hatsuye's birth, the Ogatas were evicted from their room. They fled to the lodgings of a friend, taking only what they could carry. Their bedding and most of the rest of their things, shabby as they were, had been left behind as surety for payment of their accumulated rent. Their friend was a bachelor, but when it came to empty purses he was in much the same boat as the Ogatas.

'Outrageous,' he said, 'being evicted with Yoshiye so advanced in her pregnancy! Fine. Stay as long as you like — just imagine you're on a huge luxury liner.'

He lived on the third floor in a garret-like room. Indeed, the slightest breeze made the ramshackle boarding house pitch like a huge liner.

Another friend, hearing of the Ogatas' crisis, went around collecting contributions. When he brought over what he had managed to collect he said, 'If it's not enough I'll scrape up some more.'

They managed with it. Yoshiye was delivered without complications in the spotless room of a maternity hospital. Immediately after, the Ogatas were able to move into a small house.

One friend said of Hatsuye: 'Well, Ogata, at least you've come up with one masterpiece from among all the stuff you've produced.' Ogata couldn't possibly contest that judgement.

Hatsuye's birth drove him to make a sincere reevaluation of his shiftlessness. Here he was with a wife and now a daughter. He had managed these run-of-the-mill accomplishments with a run-of-the-mill expression on his face, and yet he had failed to achieve anything in his work. Although his resistance to convention had presumably stemmed from a desire to write what he pleased, he hadn't produced much at all. His resistance had merely set him spinning round and round without getting anywhere. But now, with his resistance subsiding, he had become a conventional husband, a conventional father ....

Ogata lapsed into a state of self-disgust. Soon he started trying to depict that disgust in his writings, and little by little produced some manuscripts that earned him nothing.

He was horribly poor. He detested poverty. And yet being poverty-stricken became his one crumb of comfort.

'I'm not reaping any benefits from society,' he thought; 'I'm not pulling off any clever deals.' The idea that his motives were pure barely kept his head above water and had the bizarre effect of making him proud of his poverty.

Yoshiye seemingly suffered from it. In the final analysis, Ogata had been pulling the wool over her eyes. Not that his methods of deception were all that cunning; very simply, Yoshiye was easily fooled. His poverty had caused even more suffering for the baby, who had no recollection, was not even aware of it, because until Haysuye was about ten she never enjoyed good health. Certainly the impoverishment of those days had cast a dark shadow over her babyhood.

Three years after Hatsuye, their son, Akio, arrived. And six years after that their second daughter, Sadako, was born. Both were robust children. In fact Sadako might be called the picture of health. Ogata could not help being amazed when he looked at them now: twenty-three, twenty-one, and fifteen.

He was impressed with how well they had grown up. He didn't have the feeling he had raised them. He felt rather that they had grown up on their own. This seemed particularly true of Hatsuye.

She was often sick when she was small. When she was two or three the Ogatas' childless neighbours adored her and enjoyed 'borrowing' her. She was often taken next door because it was good for Yoshiye to have her out from underfoot. Ogata's wife never handed their daughter over without warning the neighbour lady about the child's diet or reminding her not to give the girl this or that food.

But something Hatsuye ate next door disagreed with her and she came down with infant cholera. The doctor injected the poor girl with Ringer's solution and glucose, such huge shots it looked like a rubber ball had grown on her little thigh. Somehow or other she pulled through, but her digestive tract had been vulnerable ever since, and she was still susceptible to colds. She became skinny and turned quite pale, too. Even at twenty-three she remained on the slight side, her complexion excessively pallid. Ogata felt depressed whenever he looked at her.

'Hatsuye, how about another helping?'

'What?'

'I'm asking if you would like a little more rice or something.' He only seemed indignant; he wasn't.

Looking at her mother, Hatsuye said, 'But I've already had too much to eat, haven't I, mum?'

'Hatsuye eats loads these days — even more than Sadako.'

'Really?'

'Look at the buttons on her skirt,' Mrs Ogata said, patting her daughter's hip. 'They're ready to pop.'

'I see. What's your weight?'

'Ninety-nine pounds.'

'On the light side, isn't it? Nintey-nine at five-foot-two — you've got to put on another sixteen pounds or so. Sadako's the same height and weighs about eight-and-a-half, doesn't she?'

'But that's just the way I'm constituted.'

Ogata said nothing. 'How on earth constituted,' he thought; what does that mean?

— 5 —

In mid-March of the following year, Ogata and Hatsuye went to Tokyo the day before the rites. Since her fiancé lived there, that is where the ceremony would be held. They had scheduled it for 11.30 a.m. It would be impossible to get everything in order that early if they went the same day, so Ogata decided to leave the day before; he made arrangements to stay over at the home of a friend who had agreed to help out.

Hatsuye went to the beauty parlour in a department store. She said she would do a little shopping while she was there. Ogata had become busier and busier as the day of the wedding approached; as a result, he had caught a cold. He asked his friend, therefore, to lay out his quilts and he rested.

Hatsuye returned around seven. After she showed her father her hair-do, she said, 'I'd like to have a dress rehearsal.' She meant she wanted to try on the accessories she would wear with her wedding gown.

'You'd better get to bed early tonight.'

'It'll only take half an hour or so,' she said. 'It would be terrible if I left something out ....'

'I suppose you're right. But try to be quick about it.'

'All right.'

She wasn't very quick about it, however. First of all, she set out all of her accessories and examined them one by one. And there were quite a few. She felt lost when she had to choose between two possibilities. To make matters worse, she asked her father's advice whenever she was in doubt about something. Since he had never bothered his head about such things, he didn't give the question a moment's thought before agreeing, 'That's fine!'

After she had got everything together, she began trying things on one by one. Ogata wondered why she couldn't put on a bit more weight. He felt like telling Hatsuye, so completely absorbed in trying on her things, that these baubles were not important ....

And then Ogata reviewed one after the other his memories of Hatsuye's birth, her childhood, the war years, her college days. Dredging up the past made it difficult for him to accept the fact that this girl putting her trousseau in order was the Hatsuye of those memories.

Whenever his son, Akio, came home from Tokyo where he had a room, Ogata knew that his wife's facial expression and tone of voice — but particularly her voice — would change. Yoshiye knew as well as her husband that she should not play favourites among the children, and yet she didn't know how to conceal her attitude towards Akio. It was not quite a matter of concealment. Her feelings surfaced naturally. Akio liked his mother. In the same way, Hatsuye seemed to be fond of her father. What that European psychologist had to say about these relationships, Ogata thought, was quite true.

Did these factors exist in his feelings for Hatsuye? He imagined they did.

Associated with this general complex of emotional ties between parent and child was the special feeling Ogata had for Hatsuye. At the same time that his heart went out to her, he felt anguished by pangs of guilt that stemmed from the way he had discharged his parental rôle — both at her birth and when she was still a little girl.

There's nothing I can do about it now, Ogata thought, all the more ready to reproach himself.

These feelings did not derive simply from a father-daughter relationship. He had never experienced such curious sentiments towards his younger daughter, Sadako. When she was small they were somewhat better off, still dreadfully poor but nothing like as bad as when Hatsuye was little. Though now only in junior high, Sadako stood over five-foot two and weighed eight-and-a-half stone. Proof enough, Ogata thought, of the difference between their poverty levels. Hatsuye with her slight build, her gentleness, her diligence, was overwhelmed in everything by her younger sister, nine years her junior — that carefree, self-indulgent, willful Sadako who so hated studying. Hatsuye could by no means match her sister's sheer bulk.

More than half an hour had passed since Hatsuye began trying on her things, checking their effect in the mirror, fussing here and there with them.

'Come on!' Ogata said. 'That's enough.'

Hatsuye meticulously put each item away as she took it off. She was much too meticulous. In fact, he had lectured her constantly for being fastidious to a fault. At length she finished, laid out her quilts, and changed into her night-clothes.

Ogata was suddenly overwhelmed by the thought: Tonight is the last time I'll be sleeping next to her like this. Though aware he was being maudlin, he had no inclination to quash his feelings.

'Hatsuye-chan!' Ogata addressed her as he had ever since she was a baby. 'This really is goodbye, isn't it?'

She nodded in agreement, looking at her father with a smile

that rapidly melted into tears. The overflow from both eyes in no time began trickling past her nostrils.

'Don't cry. Your eyes will look ghastly tomorrow.'

Hatsuye hung her head, holding her sleeves to her eyes. Ogata had nothing to say. No, he thought of many things to say: 'You're sincere but not shrewd. I can't say your constitution is the best. Pay more attention to these things.'

Or, 'I wish I didn't have to let you get married.'

But the former seemed idiotic and the latter self-indulgent.

'Go and refresh your eyes at the sink,' he said in a peremptory tone.

Hatsuye nodded and got up. Shortly after, she returned with a wet towel, an embarrassed expression on her face.

Ogata opened his briefcase and took out the sleeping pills he used from time to time. 'Take some of these and go to bed. You've never taken sleeping pills before, have you?'

'Never'.

'Well, four should be plenty. I need seven.'

'Do you think it's all right?'

'What's all right?'

'You don't think I'll oversleep, do you?'

'If you oversleep, I'll wake you.'

Hatsuye took the pills, though with a curious look on her face. Ogata swallowed his after making sure she had swallowed hers.

— 6 —

The next day, the day of the nuptials, Ogata's wife, son and other daughter came up from the country and met him at the hotel where the ceremony would be held. Ogata changed into the *kimono* his wife had brought along, the one with the family crests. His weariness had made his cold take a slight turn for the worse and he felt extremely lethargic.

The ceremony went as planned. The couple in gown and morning suit looked a bit quaint listening so reverently to the priest who read the Shinto rituals.

But Hatsuye was unimaginably beautiful in her white wedding gown. The mere sight of her somehow bolstered Ogata's spirits.

After a brief interlude it was time for the reception. Counting friends and relatives on both sides, sixty people attended.

A number of people Hatsuye had known since childhood rose and offered congratulatory messages. Ogata cupped his hand to an ear, eagerly straining to hear their speeches, so difficult to catch because the microphone did not work properly. Each message contained something that moved him. But he didn't find those anecdotes very funny that everyone else thought so amusing.

Dr T. had saved Hatsuye's life when she was a little girl. He rose and said, 'After Hatsuye recovered from cholera I was asked to help celebrate. This marks the second celebration I'm attending. I hope to officiate soon at the third — a blessed event.' Everyone clapped. Ogata only stared at the table.

Then a friend's daughter who had married six months earlier stood up. His friend, who shared the same family name, had christened his daughter Hatsuye, too. Since the girls were the same age and in the same department at college, there were amusing tales about how from time to time, people had mistaken one Ogata Hatsuye for the other.

'Since I married a step ahead of her and am now Ōmura Hatsuye, I felt relieved to think that people would no longer mix us up. But when I heard that Hatsuye was getting married I began to worry. What if she became Mrs Ōmura too? But since she's Mrs Furuya I can relax now. Congratulations!'

A ripple of laughter accompanied the brisk applause that greeted her remarks. This time even Ogata could laugh. He, his wife, and Hatsuye had been invited to this girl's wedding reception and Hatsuye had been chosen to hand the bride her bouquet.

Soon the dinner was over. Hatsuye, who had by then changed into her going-away clothes, accepted a bouquet from the daughter of one of her mother's friends. Then she and the groom left for the station, which was next to the hotel. Of course, Mrs Ogata, Akio, and Sadako, as well as a number of Hatsuye's friends, went along to see the couple off.

Ogata dragged his listless frame to the floor above, where he entered an ante-room attached to the wedding hall. Finding himself alone he stretched out on one of the couches, formal attire and all, and shut his eyes. Shortly after, the weary Ogata realised that he could see the western edge of Tokyo Station from that side of the hotel, so he went over and sat down by the window.

He looked at his watch. Nearly three.

The train's about to leave, he thought. I suppose they're taking the Ideyu Express. I should be able to see it from here. As he watched to see which platform the express would be leaving from, he heard the departure bell. The train on the furthest track began to move. It stretched out smoothly, gradually gathering momentum. Soon he could see the specially-marked reserved coach.

That's the one they're on, he thought.

Ogata stared blankly at the train as it pulled away. Suddenly he felt empty. And a bit sad.

That Hatsuye of mine — what'll she do with her bouquet? Forget it? Abandon it? Take it along to the inn?

He had forced this thought about the bouquet to shake off his emptiness, his sadness.

(JUNE 1957)

10

Putting in for Retirement

— 1 —

'You're getting deaf,' my wife said.

'Yup, getting deaf,' I answered without hesitation.

That exchange occurred because I missed something she had said to me from the next room. I was listening to the news on the radio. Instead of repeating what she had said, my wife merely stated with some decisiveness that I was getting deaf and left it at that. I simply responded that she was right and turned back to the news.

The programme ended in another two or three minutes. Switching off the radio, I asked her, 'What was that all about?'

'All what?'

'What did you say to me just now?'

'That? … Oh … I forget.'

It didn't seem to matter to her, so it didn't matter to me either.

Although I haven't quite become deaf, I admit that I no longer hear as well as I once did. About a year ago I became aware that my hearing was not what it used to be. And a year before I realised my memory was deteriorating, though I never admitted it openly.

In my youth I was a lackadaisical bum, a lazy, apathetic individual. I enthusiastically involved myself in whatever struck my fancy, but never became the least interested in anything that did not.

'It's a pain!' was a favourite phrase of mine during my twenties.

At twenty, however, the death of my father saddled me with looking after my mother and the four younger children. Since, in the eyes of society, I was the family head, there were social duties to perform whether I cared to or not. It was around the end of World War I, a time when people still strictly adhered to cherished conventions; my family, moreover, had long-established roots in the country, which was more conservative than elsewhere.

I continually dismissed whatever failed to interest me with the phrase, 'It's a pain!' Actually, that was a dubious way to deal with problems. I never cared how things turned out as long as I had managed to 'dismiss' them. Thus, I either took care of the problem at one stroke, clean as a whistle, or left it be and ignored it altogether. If I left it alone, sooner or later it resolved itself. More often than not, however, the result was unfavourable.

Once, when I was twenty-four or twenty-five and still in college, I was out strolling with a couple of friends. I walked a pace or so ahead, dangling a cigarette from my lips, hands shoved into my pockets. Though small and wiry, whenever I walked with somebody I invariably led the way. I just happened to be a fast walker. It was, I'm sure, a habit acquired during my five years in middle school when I had to commute nearly ten miles on foot each day.

The wind had blown some ash off my cigarette and one small live particle ended up on the bridge of my nose. It felt hot. But thinking that it was nothing, that it would go out straight away, I never bothered brushing it off. It would have been too much trouble to take a hand out of my pocket.

The ash did go out, though somewhat more slowly than I anticipated, leaving a small blister on my nose.

I dredge up this trivial matter from forty years back, satisfied that it typifies perfectly the apathy that characterised me then.

— 2 —

I rather suspect that I'm still a novice, both as a human being and as a member of society. I became aware of this when I turned sixty-four.

Needless to say, I'm not exactly sure in this context what it means to be an 'expert' as opposed to a 'novice.' Still, I haven't the slightest doubt that these categories exist. The words 'unskilled' and 'skilled' come to mind, but though they resemble what I sense in the words 'novice' or 'expert,' they seem somewhat different.

Yearbooks and the like list my profession as 'writer' or 'author.' These days I'm more or less accustomed to that, but the truth is that I don't feel these words quite describe what I'm doing. It's not as though I'm involved in something else, so if it's a matter of describing my work, I suppose I'll leave it at that.

Yet it's a fact that I have constant doubts about calling myself an author or novelist — or, rather, about even thinking of myself in those terms.

(There is no mistaking the fact that I make my living by writing pieces and selling them to newspapers and magazines. Simply put, the problem is the nature of these writings. My compositions — I don't know if they're what people think of as stories. Merely because

I have been fortunate enough to have people treat me as an author I strive to make a living by more or less putting on the appearance that I am an author — But how should I respond to someone who might question whether I am one? I have yet to be challenged on that by anyone, but I constantly ask myself how I might answer if I were. Isn't it about time I came up with a clear answer? But no. That's much too rash a way to deal with it. Nor will it do to say, 'Damn, it's a pain,' and arbitrarily round off all the numbers. I've got to take some time and organise things.)

Organisation.

Over the past few years I've been thinking of little else. I haven't got a thing in place. Nor have I the slightest idea yet what goes where.

I conceive of 'organisation' as putting things in order, making things coherent, as seeing for the first time, Aha! so that's how it fits. I'm using the term in the sense that includes everything concrete and abstract.

From long experience, I've learned that the best way to keep things from getting all jammed up is to relentlessly tackle each task as it presents itself. In recent years I've been using this method with some degree of success in dealing with everyday trifles. The best example is how I answer my mail. I make it a practice to respond immediately to any communication that requires an answer. When I fail to write at once, I cannot seem to get the letter off and ultimately fail to acknowledge the note despite my best intentions. It wouldn't be so bad if I were only deficient in good manners, but sometimes in the conduct of my daily life I incur major losses for myself and others.

Long ago, when I was around thirty and lived in Tokyo, I received mail from my mother in Shimosoga, where I now live. For a time I burnt every letter, never opening a single one. I had declared to her that I would be a scoundrel and I took delight in acting that way. It wasn't only towards my mother, either; I completely spurned my brothers and sisters as well.

Then, before I knew it, all the family property — put up for surety on loans I had made — had been auctioned away. Later on, I asked what had happened and found that mother's frequent letters had reported the impending auction. She had demanded that I deal with the crisis. Apart from blistering my nose and forfeiting our family estate, my 'let-it-be-ism' caused improprieties too numerous to list. As a result, I ended up having the townsfolk honour me with the designation, 'that scandalous Ogata boy.'

Yet I don't think of myself as particularly deficient in the sense of responsibility. Ever since I was a child I had been strictly brought up to be the 'successor' to an old House. In the spring of my twentieth year, when I lost my father, I felt every inch the heir and audaciously expected that I could manage my affairs flawlessly and keep mother and the other children in line — all of them inexperienced in the ways of the world. But since the heir himself totally lacked experience in the ways of the world, such expectations were absurd. Not a single thing turned out as I had hoped, so I came to the view that — what the hell — nothing was that important and decided I might just as well run full tilt in the opposite direction.

I had shrugged off and rejected all my responsibilities as the son and heir. But having taken a wife and fathered a daughter, I felt like taking the initiative and assuming my responsibilities as a husband and father. I told myself that I had rejoined the human race. Even my old and disgusting habit of occasionally acting the scoundrel began to disappear little by little as a result of my efforts, and I flatter myself that, after spending four or five years around the end of World War II flat on my back convalescing in my native village, I was almost able to become an average family man.

— 3 —

Four or five years flat on my back convalescing! I can say that now that I have more or less regained my health, but the truth is that my recuperation has been faster than I expected. My condition became critical in the August of my forty-fourth year, exactly twenty years ago. I made up my own five-year plans for survival, but by the time I got through my first two I wasn't much in the mood anymore for making a third one. I mean, I had changed my mind about long-term plans and came to believe that I would be ahead if only I lived through another day. And then, shortly after turning sixty, I became aware that my memory was failing. I've also noted for the past year or so that my hearing has been getting worse.

While listening to the radio I frequently either have my nose in the newspaper or respond to the wife or daughter. So when I reproached our youngest for habitually studying with the radio on, she shot back with, 'But daddy, you're a "same-timer" too.'

'You don't say? Do we have such an expression now?'

'Come on, dad, don't go laying a smoke screen to evade the issue.'

'I'm not evading the issue. You're doing your studies, right? I'm merely reading the newspaper.'

'I study better with background music.'

'Really ...?'

I suddenly recalled then how, during my twenties, I constantly found myself improvising melodies in my head to accompany the short pieces I wrote. (This may differ from what my daughter had in mind, but there's probably a connection there somewhere. Or is there? Well, whatever, later on rhythms and melodies no longer popped into my head as I was writing. Does that mean I've lost something?) Because my thoughts had taken this twist, that was the end of the 'same-timer' incident ....

My wife's statement, 'You're getting deaf,' had a tinge of firmness. I sensed that she knew I had no reason to refute her statement. I responded without giving it a thought, acting as though she was right; I hadn't the slightest desire to tack on any if's, and's, or but's.

My wife didn't say another word about my hearing. I don't suppose she had forgotten about it. For myself, since I remained conscious enough of the incident to write it up, I became interested in surmising how she later felt about it. I felt it would be odd to ask her directly, so I tried to think from various angles how she might have looked at it.

But when you boil it all down, what she probably meant was, 'So it's finally caught up with you, too, has it?' And since I guessed it had, my response meant, 'You're right — sad to say.' After all, what else could either of us have said? And what could we do about it?

— 4 —

My elder daughter is thirty-one, married with two children. My son is twenty-nine; married, he also has two children. Both are independent and not the slightest burden on their parents. Our only concern is their health and the health of their families. We had a second son who died at three months, not a problem for us now because it happened twenty-five years ago. Our younger daughter graduated from college this March and went to work for a newspaper. She turned twenty-three in early June of this year. She's single.

Thus, as you can see, the only task left to me as a father is to map out the future of this younger daughter.

I am quite impressed by the way I've bumbled along so well up to this point. Looking around me, the business of parenting seems utterly commonplace, so what do I have to brag about? Everybody nurtures a child till it manages to strike out on its own. But, when I look back on my record as a father I cannot resist feeling good about that much, at least. I think there are good reasons why I might be impressed by and rejoice over something that is, objectively speaking, all too commonplace.

Until the early 1930s, the generally-accepted notion in Japanese society was that anyone who set his heart on literature automatically set his heart on poverty. Perhaps today's youth may not be able to comprehend this, but anyone beyond middle age will, I think, nod his head in agreement. I have no intention here of arguing for or against the reasonableness of this attitude. Nor do I intend to grumble about the social order that supported such a notion.

I had made up my mind to become a writer around the end of World War I. In those days, any aspiring writer confronted the popular notion that writing literature guaranteed poverty. This attitude showed no signs of waning, so anyone setting his heart on literature in that milieu took the first step towards his goal with this reality in mind.

The majority gave up along the way. Those who held out starved to death. Only an extremely small number of the talented went on to win fame, and even most of them died before their time.

Ignoring the rightness or wrongness of the writer's commitment to — or the social conventions that forced the writer into — poverty, the fact is that I joined those who under these conditions dedicated themselves to writing.

Although lacking talent, I held on, refusing to give up (or rather, I suppose, I had little choice in the matter). And so I ended up flirting with death. It was a disconcerting thought. But on the other hand, since I would only be lying in the bed I had made, I was able to resign myself to my fate.

Ill as I was, I did recover after spending four to five years on my back. I am grateful for that.

Aside from my own survival, the situation for writers changed in the post-World War II era. People welcomed fiction and reading material with enormous enthusiasm. The so-called vogue writers appeared in droves. My writings have never been much in demand because I cannot produce pieces that fit the current fashion. But like aftershocks from a distant quake, the new situation touched me with its benefits, small as they may have been.

My younger daughter was three in 1945, the year the war ended. Formations of carrier-based Grumman fighters, coming in from Sagami Bay to make their raids, winged over near the summit of Mt Soga behind our house. They swooped down to strafe the train station and private homes at the foot of the mountain. They hit ours too. I could see the white scarf fluttering from the neck of each enemy pilot. I could hear machine-gun bullets and empty cartridges ricochet with sharp pings off the rocks in our garden. Then the screams of my younger daughter, frightened out of her wits.

And in those years right after the war everything went extremely badly for me.

The year my younger daughter reached her majority at the age of twenty, our city's Education Commission invited me to the public ceremony honouring those who had officially become adults. I attended and said a few congratulatory words. When I looked out from the rostrum at all those young men and women my daughter's age — basically boys and girls in adult bodies, their faces exuding vitality — I felt so touched that the words caught in my throat. Also interfering with what I intended to say were various scenes from the last days of the war that drifted through my mind. Strafing that rattled our *shōji* doors. Bullets ricocheting off the rocks. The hour-long succession of exploding artillery shells our army had stashed in the local train depot. The indescribable sound of metal ripping through our roof and floor before biting with a clank into the ground. The screams of our little one. The almost unbelievable blue of the sky after the enemy planes flew off. The green of the trees outside my window. The red and white of the flowers.

As I watched from my sick-bed, the line between reality and unreality blurred. Then, all of a sudden, I heard the voice of my three-year-old daughter. She was singing her favourite, the naval air cadet song. The way her penetrating voice stumbled through the melody deeply moved the depleted spirits of this invalid. With no one watching, I wasn't ashamed to let the tears flow ....

These scenes loomed before my mind's eye, blocking what I'd planned to tell these young people. I said simply that, to boil it all down, I was grateful that they had managed to grow up so nicely. Then I stepped down from the dais. Since many city officials and parents were present, I managed to make some reference to 'the efforts and pains of parents and teachers.' But in the main I clearly put the stress on the young people: 'You've all managed so well to survive, to become adults!' At the dinner table that evening my daughter said, 'Dad, you were different today.' I inferred from her remark that my talk appeared to have been quite introspective.

— 5 —

I must mention something that happened to me the other day when I went up to Tokyo, dragged my daughter away from her job, and went shopping in the Ginza area. It's not that anything special happened, but for me it was a memorable day.

Generally speaking, I hate going to Tokyo. Over the last three or four years I have written a number of articles about my distaste, so it's wearisome to repeat myself. In a word, I hate it because Tokyo is such an ecological disaster area.

I arrive at Shinbashi Station some hour-and-a-half or so after changing to the Shōnan Line at Kōzu. As one nears Yokohama, the air turns foul. By the time I get off at Shinbashi or Tokyo, my sense of smell has been somewhat dulled by the pollution, and yet from time to time I get a whiff of particularly rank air.

After waiting in a taxi for the third light before getting through an intersection, I can no longer endure the stench of the exhaust fumes. I feel sick to the stomach. My head aches. At times I abandon my taxi and escape into a nearby coffee shop. Once inside, there's the strident clamour of the jazz ....

People who live in Tokyo may not understand my distaste. But somebody like myself who has lived in the countryside for some twenty years, a person who lives away from the din in a place with clean air, pure water, and greenery, can only think of Tokyo as a cesspool. I had become a fresh-water fish. How, then, could I possibly be expected to breathe in Tokyo's excessively 'salty' environment?

I attend various meetings there only if it is imperative that I go. When it's something like a party, I generally leave before the end.

Whenever I go to Tokyo, moreover, I try to lump together a number of chores and dispose of them on the same trip. I skilfully line up the tasks I must attend to and make a list. That's why I am understandably in such a flurry during the time I'm in the city.

That's how it was the other day, too. I made the rounds, stopping off at three different places. Then, after I'd finished my business, I dragged my daughter away from her work around three in the afternoon. The objective was to get her to accompany me on a shopping trip so that I could buy a tie and some shoes. I had submitted to the opinions of wife and daughter who said they were concerned about the kind of items I might buy. I personally have no confidence in such matters and so ... in any event, since when it comes to shopping I tend to buy the very first thing I set my eyes on, I thought it best to let my daughter make the choices.

She hauled me around to three or four stores. That was annoying, but I could only grin and bear it in view of the fact that I'd put her in charge of the buying. Finally, we finished (in the process she got me to buy her a pair of shoes, too) and I suddenly brightened up at the prospect of getting out of that cesspool. I hailed a taxi, saw my daughter back to where she works, and had the cab take me on to Tokyo Station. I hurried up to the platform just in time to catch a train which coincided perfectly with the Gotenba Line at Kōzu. I was gasping for breath but content with having caught a train with such convenient connections.

My wife came to the entrance-way of our house. 'You're home already?' she said. 'My, that was quick!'

'The train connections were perfect,' I said a bit apologetically.

'And Keichan?'

'She said she has some work left. She'll probably be coming in on the second train after mine.'

I had no reason to rush, yet I hurriedly pulled off my clothing. My wife ran around after me picking it all up.

'Have you had supper yet?'

'Not yet,' I said.

Then she said with a touch of disappointment in her voice, 'I thought maybe you'd be eating out somewhere with Keichan. I don't have a thing in the house.'

'That's all right. Just hurry and fix me a bottle of *sake.*'

I had the feeling that the more Tokyo air I breathed the worse it would be for me, so the moment I finish my business I escape to the countryside. If the apricot trees are in full bloom when I get off the train at Shimosoga's little local station, the perfume of apricot blossoms greets me. If tangerines are in bloom, it's their aroma.

My wife finds it annoying when I come home early since I so rarely leave the house. I was aware of how she felt, but I hadn't the slightest inclination to wander around Tokyo just because of that.

Sometimes I say to her, 'Sorry — I'm back.'

That evening, as I had guessed, my daughter came in on the second train after mine, bringing what we had picked up on our shopping trip. She laid out everything and for a time fussed about, including trying on her new shoes.

In the process she said, 'It's no fun shopping with dad. It's always rush, rush, rush.'

'You're so right,' my wife was quick to sympathise. 'That's how he's been for years and years.'

'That's because I'm not interested in shopping the way you girls are. Old books excepted, of course.'

'O.K., we're interested in shopping,' Keiko said. 'But it's not necessarily just an interest. It's a matter of carefully selecting the right article.'

'So you combine interest with utility? That's great. It's just that you'll have to count me out.'

I said it lightheartedly, but my daughter responded with a serious look.

'Father, you're too impatient. Whether going up or down the steps in the station, crossing the street or whatever, I think you should take it easier.' When she said that, I felt I had to respond.

'The reason I'm impatient, you know, is that when I go up to Tokyo I always have a lot of things to attend to. Naturally I end up bustling around.'

'Maybe so, but it's scary. Merely watching you makes me jittery.'

'Hmmph. It's really that scary, is it? ... Do I totter along so?' I'd already wiped the grin off my face.

'Tottering along — that's not what I'm talking about. Today, for instance, when you hailed a cab in the Ginza area you dashed right out into the street. It scared me silly. I could flag down the cab myself. If that's how you're going to be, I feel like refusing to go anywhere with you.'

She was relentless. I glared back at her, wondering how she could talk to her father like that. Moments later I said, 'O.K. I understand.'

My wife and daughter suddenly looked non-plussed. Then they apparently felt like sympathising with me.

'Things like climbing trees — that's absolutely out, I suppose,' my wife said as though to smooth my feathers.

'What do you mean, "out?" I'll do it when you're not around .... Come on, get the shoes and things put away.'

That was their cue to gather everything up and lug it into the next room, where they began opening and closing drawers.

I kept pondering the reasons for having nodded so agreeably and saying, 'O.K. I understand.' I'd had the vague impression that it was just about time for me to retire from active life, but now I knew for sure. The time had come.

Some sixteen years earlier I had written a short piece called, 'The Skinny Rooster.' In those days around the end of 1948 I was an invalid with no assurance of recovery. That was the tail end of the first of several five-year plans for my survival that I had set up unknown to my family.

Confined to bed, I had little to do but watch our neighbour's chickens. I corroborated then my discovery that a rooster manifests a typically patriarchal attitude. The way he struts and fusses as he attends his brood is disagreeably paternalistic and bossy. From my perspective, moreover, his solemn over-reactions to trifling incidents struck me as terribly ludicrous.

I smiled wryly, for I could see my own behaviour reflected perfectly in his. Looking back, I realise that once I had married and fathered a child I told myself I would rejoin the human race. I had, in a word, decided then to assign myself the rôle of the rooster of my brood. But I completely lacked the capacity to match this weighty decision. And so, day and night, I merely flailed wildly about and, consequently, the more serious I became about playing my rôle the less able I was to appreciate how ludicrous it all was.

Even as I flailed about, however, this skin-and-bone rooster somehow approached his hoped-for goals. He had raised the two older children and seen them become independent. Her education completed, he had got his younger daughter a job. It remained only to find her an appropriate spouse, though that might even be left up to her ....

(Say, Keichan, your earlier remarks were quite to the point. Come to think of it, your timing was perfect. I see what you mean, and so I've decided that starting now I'll be converted, like a Mr Hyde becoming a Dr Jekyll. Since I've been such a meddler, I'll make it a point to stop backing you up every time a ball comes your way. Perhaps then you'll not let grounders zip between your legs or fumble or throw wild when you take the field. And when the ball bounds over the outfield fence, go chase it yourself. Don't fret about being a run or two behind. Get a hit and earn them back — Now that I think of it, at your age your mother already had two babies ....)

I called loudly to the two of them; they were folding clothes in the next room. 'Now's as good an opportunity as ever. It's high time I decided to stop trying to run her life for her.'

'What's that ...? You'll stop what?'

'Well, I've been thinking. I'm tired of it myself. And besides, Keichan's a big girl now ....'

They simultaneously broke into laughter.

'You think we're picking on you.' This from my wife.

'That's not what I had in mind.' This from my daughter.

'I don't think you're picking on me at all,' I said. 'I just thought, yes, you're right .... Get on with it, but don't come complaining to me.'

'Dad, I'm speechless ... um, I humbly entreat you henceforth that I might respectfully continue receiving your magnanimous patronage ....'

'I get the point.'

Two days after the new order went into effect I went up to Tokyo again. As was my custom, I did the two or three jobs I had to do — finally stopping off at the company where Keiko works. I had something to discuss with several of the executives, but I dealt with that in about half an hour and asked them to send my daughter in. I didn't have anything special to say to her, I just wanted to see her for a moment. When she appeared I took her down to the first floor.

'Can you leave yet?' I asked.

'I'm in the middle of something right now. In another hour or so.'

'Well, I guess you can't make it then.'

'Can't make what?'

'I just thought we could stop off at that place in Shinbashi and have supper together on our way home.'

'Gosh, I am sorry,' she said.

'Can you spare ten minutes now?'

'Certainly.'

We went to a tea-room on the ground floor. I told her, 'Order anything you want.'

Shortly afterwards as we walked towards the main entrance I said, 'Get me a cab, will you?'

'Yes, of course.'

She nimbly went out of the entrance-way, skillfully flagged down a passing cab, stood by the door and ushered me into the back seat with mock solemnity. I intentionally boarded with unruffled poise, held my head high, and raised my hand in a greatly affected manner. My daughter stood in the wake of the departing taxi with the deferential pose of one who had just seen off a V.I.P.

For some time now it has been my habit to leave things up to my son whenever I go anywhere with him. Buying the evening paper, getting train tickets, hailing taxis — I leave all such tasks to him. I never try to walk on ahead of him. I've been able to feel at ease in using him as an aide, so to speak. Indeed, from the outset my son has been dependability itself. If I asked him to mail a post-card on the way to school, he would post it without fail. If I asked him to deliver a manuscript or something to a newspaper or magazine, he carried out the task flawlessly. He never lost things, never had his pocket picked. That's why I can say that by nature he has the makings of a good aide.

By contrast, I haven't the slightest confidence in my younger daughter to do any of those tasks (the same goes for my wife, too, but that's another matter). The post-card I ask her to post for me turns up in her purse two or three days later. Time and again pickpockets take the wallet from her handbag. If I give her some money and ask her to do some shopping for me, she often forgets to do it. And when she does come back with what she bought, she makes no effort to return my change. You may wonder whether she means to pocket it for herself. She doesn't. She's simply completely absent-minded.

And so in my dealings with Keiko I had no choice. I became her aide. Since on various occasions she lets grounders slip through her fingers, muffs catches, and throws wild balls, I get all hot and bothered running around trying to back her up.

'Why not just leave her alone sometimes?' my wife would say.

'I'd very much like to,' I answer, 'but I know I'll be in trouble if I do.'

'Basically, she's a selfish shirk.'

'She's a shirk, she's very cunning, too.'

'I'm sure she's got guts, though,' my wife said. 'I can't light a candle to her on that score.'

'You're probably right.'

In most cases my wife then adds something to this effect: 'And besides you really do spoil her. You're as soft as a cream puff.' From that point on we get involved in a kind of familial town-hall scene.

But I suppose I won't have to worry any more about such

discussions. After all, I've stopped being Keiko's aide and have decided instead to use her as mine.

Seeing her father poking into all her affairs and, despite his age, running around like a demented cockerel, there must be times when Keiko gets scared silly and wants to shout, 'Mind how you go, dad!' And there must be times when she finds her father's behaviour unbecoming and gets fed up with him. I can't prevent a wry smile from stealing over my face when such thoughts come to mind.

— 6 —

Put simply, ever since I rejoined the human race I've been trying to have my cake and eat it. If I can stop acting as my younger daughter's aide, then I will end up having my cake. But it's been my secret ambition to presume to eat it as well.

It's a matter of hoping that somehow or other I will be able to realise the things I've set my heart on accomplishing for so many years without, at the same time, relaxing my pose as the average husband and father. Those involved in work like mine will certainly understand at once the difficulty of pursuing both objectives, but I don't suppose that the average person will be able to see my point at all.

Twenty years ago on my sick-bed I heard not only Keiko's petrified shrieks as she reacted to the strafing of the enemy Grumman fighters, but also the naval air cadet song that she sang in her penetrating yet stumbling way. My relationship with my younger daughter has always been coloured by such images. And then, most recently, Keiko's complaints about me (which could also have meant something like, 'Leave me alone!') combined with my wife's remarks about my hearing (which could possibly translate into something like, 'You don't have many years left, do you?') led me to think — if I may exaggerate — that the scales had just fallen from my eyes.

It was an excellent opportunity to rid myself of my rôle as the rooster around here. I'd certainly like to retire from this particular job. Thanks to my having been trained since childhood to become a rooster, I've been overplaying that part for quite some time now. But now it's no longer necessary to behave in such a ridiculous manner, because as far as I'm concerned I have, for all practical purposes, already had my cake.

★   ★   ★

Setting up the children in life has been one of the hardest rôles in my rooster career. But nothing gratifies me more than finding that I've more or less managed it. I'm certainly thankful for that. And I'd like to have this confession taken at face value.

From here on in, I'm going to get on with organising the rest of my life. I'll organise things in one fell swoop: the old magazines, books, and things stacked in my study; my old letters; old photographs; the old papers inherited from my father — it's a matter of beginning with what's right at hand. And then, along with that, I'll go on to organise certain areas which, despite my having poked around at them for some time, haven't yet been taken care of. Such organisation is, I mean to say, a matter of getting on with my writing, though I need not add that this is the toughest task of all. However, I insist on eating my cake as well as having it. It's discouraging that my hearing has begun to go and that I don't remember things so well anymore, but now that I'm unquestionably an oldie, what can I do about it? As long as I'm clearly aware of my shortcomings, I can make greater progress in organising things — so that my shortcomings may actually be advantages.

*   *   *

An apricot thudded to the ground.

'Oh, that reminds me ...' 'my wife said with her scatter-brained squeak.

'Reminds you of what?'

'Of what I said to you during the midday news. You know, you asked me about it afterwards.'

'You mean the time I didn't hear you?'

'Yes. I said it's about time to knock the apricots off the tree. Look, another one has just dropped off.'

'Great! Let's go and knock them all down.'

'Right now ...?' she asked with a terribly annoyed look.

'Best to get it done the moment you think of it.' I stood up.

Getting up begrudgingly, she said, 'What's the big hurry?' It sounded as though she was mumbling to herself. Pretending I hadn't heard, I headed into the yard from the verandah.

(AUGUST 1964)